S0-BJP-143

BEGINNINGS IN THEOLOGY

BEGINNINGS IN THEOLOGY

BY

JACK FINEGAN

ASSOCIATION PRESS *New York*

BEGINNINGS IN THEOLOGY

ASSOCIATION PRESS, 291 BROADWAY, NEW YORK 7, N. Y.

LIBRARY OF CONGRESS CATALOG CARD NUMBER: 56-5029

PRINTED IN THE UNITED STATES OF AMERICA

Preface

This book is an endeavor to think seriously and write plainly about some of the central convictions of the Christian faith. In the character of its thought it reflects the increased concern of our time with theology; in the manner of its expression it is intended to be useful to all the people of the church, the "laity," as they are sometimes called, of whose importance there is also an increased realization in our day. Indeed, it is hoped that it will also be of value to people outside the church who have interest in knowing what the Christian faith is and what it has to say at the present.

Fundamentally I have tried to find out and set forth some of the important things which are told in the Bible about God, Jesus Christ, and the church, but at the same time I have endeavored to keep in mind the knowledge that man has from other sources about his universe and his life, and so have sought to bring the two together, biblical teachings and modern understanding. Some of the contemporary books which have to do with the subjects discussed are mentioned in the text or cited in the notes, and will offer possibilities for further reading if desired. For the most part the work is based directly upon the Bible, and so the primary suggestion for further investigation would be that the biblical references themselves be looked up and studied in their context. The notes will be found at the end of the book, and acknowledgments are made within them for the quotations which have been used.

JACK FINEGAN

CONTENTS

INTRODUCTION

CHAPTER ONE

The Return to Theology

G. K. Chesterton once remarked, "We have found all the questions that can be found; now we need to find the answers." Science has found out much of how the universe works, but does not profess to tell what it means. Science describes how men behave but does not pretend to say how they ought to behave. Philosophy often so emphasizes open-mindedness that we come to see many possible answers without being able to find any single one that convinces us. I was told that after a lecture on immortality by a distinguished speaker, the people who heard it knew everything there was to know about immortality except whether or not the lecturer believed in it. Now we would like to find not just questions but, in some way, answers that are convincing. In such a situation, theology has a definite role, for it is somewhat like three-dimensional photography: it is an attempt to see into the depth of things.

We have been faced in our day by the rise of powerful movements, animated by strongly held ideologies. I take it that in the secular world an ideology is much the same thing as a theology in the Christian world. An ideology is a systematic scheme of ideas about life. It is the characteristic manner and content of thought of a group of people. We know that communism has an ideology. There is no doubt that Communists have a set of ideas in which they believe, and that they think these correspond with how things really are. There is no doubt that they have convictions and are trying to convince others. How can you resist anything like that unless you yourself believe something, believe it to be the truth indeed, and believe it most strongly?

Again, in our time we have heard others than church leaders saying things which we ourselves in the churches ought to have been saying all the time. We have heard a general, standing on the deck of a battleship, say that the crisis of our time is theological. We have heard atomic scientists warning of doom and calling the world to repent. We have heard psychologists saying there is nothing in modern psychology that Jesus did not say long ago. When some of us in the churches were apologetic in the presence of the generals and the scientists and the psychologists, wondering if we even dared to mention the name of Jesus, they themselves had already begun talking of him. This means that there is a new climate of thought in our time, when it is possible to consider God and Christ and the meaning of Christianity more affirmatively than for a long time. Such, then, are some of the reasons that there is actually a return in this most recent time to the thinking about God which we call theology.

It may be hoped that the new theology will avoid

some of the errors of the old. It is to be desired that it will prove itself vital rather than technical. It may be that its words will be of more than one syllable in length, but they must always have to do with the vital concerns of man's existence. The term salvation may have three syllables, but if it is a technical expression it also has to do with a vital matter. Who does not need to be saved from his sins? Who of us has not "done those things which we ought not to have done," and "left undone those things which we ought to have done"?

The new theology may be expected to be humble. Some theological statements have sounded arrogant and presumptuous. Men have seemed to claim knowledge of matters beyond the scope of man's knowing. Yet many theologians, even in days past, have spoken with great humility. Who said, "Now we see in a mirror dimly"? That was Paul in I Corinthians 13:12, the man who was the first major theologian of the Christian movement. Who declared, "All that can be said about God is not God, but only certain smallest fragments which fall from his table"? St. Catherine of Genoa said that in the sixteenth century. Who stated, "His essence, indeed, is incomprehensible, utterly transcending all human thought"? John Calvin, doubtless the most brilliant theologian at a youthful age there ever was. Who said, "Our safest eloquence concerning him is our silence, when we confess without confession that his glory is inexplicable, his greatness above our capacity and reach. He is above, and we upon earth; therefore it behooveth our words to be wary and few"? Hooker, a great Christian leader of the sixteenth century. So, if we try to get great answers to great questions today, we must do it still with the humble recognition that God's vastness is something infinitely more than the fragment of his reality which we shall be able to understand.

Furthermore, the new theology will probably be ecumenical, general, rather than divisive. In meetings of the World Council of Churches the word "conversation" is frequently employed. They are having an "ecumenical conversation." In the World Council of Churches, representatives of the different branches of Christendom are sitting together and talking about what they believe, what they understand, and what their heritage of truth is. Thus theology is moving not toward divisiveness but toward ecumenicity.

And the new theology will be Christian, if to be Christian is to take Jesus' words for guidance and to think earnestly about what his whole life means.

CHAPTER TWO

Mystery in Religion

The difficulties of theology, however, are great. One stands here on the edge of vast mysteries. One strives to know, yet one realizes that one cannot know fully. The finite mind cannot comprehend the infinite, the limited cannot encompass the illimitable. At best, "we see in a mirror dimly."[1]

If There Were No Mystery

Yet if there were no mystery there would probably not be any religion. When we study the life of primitive man we find him doing many things which are of a common-sense, everyday sort, such as chipping a flint to make a keener cutting tool, or working up the ground so that plants will grow better. But we also find in him a sense of something more mysterious round about him. With reference to this environing mystery he sometimes practices magic, but at other times bows in reverence, and thus religion is born. In ancient civilized times the religions which were the strongest competitors of early Christianity were those known as the mystery religions. They professed to bring knowledge about mysterious things to those who believed in them. In the Bible the word mystery occurs a number of times. Jesus said to his disciples, "Unto you it is given to know the mystery of the kingdom of God," and Paul wrote, "We speak the wisdom of God in a mystery."[2] Ephesians 5:32 follows the explanation of a matter with a remark, "This is a great mystery." I Timothy 3:16 declares, "Great is the mystery of our religion." So, wherever we encounter religion, we find some sense of mystery. If everything were completely understood and made plain before our gaze, the sense of wonder might depart from our lives, since it is from this sense of something vaster than we are, that much of our faith grows.

Some years ago a famous philosopher and distinguished mathematician wrote a book on the subject of *Science and Religion.* This book gave the impression that science had now explained almost everything, and in doing so had pushed religion almost into oblivion. With just a little more time and a little more research, it seemed to say, science will explain everything, and then religion will be made completely superfluous. But at about the same time another scientist also wrote about the world and its meaning, and to his book he gave the name *The Mysterious Universe.* Thomas Edison once remarked that no man knows "the one-millionth part of anything." T. Swann Harding said, "No true scientist could explain a common pin within his lifetime, though he devoted himself exclusively to that minute object." Thus in spite of the claims of some, humility and a sense of environing mystery seem characteristic of many great scientists.

Philosophy also, at its best, seems to preserve a sense of the wonder of things, rather than to engender a feeling of sufficiency to answer every question and solve every problem. It is related that when a new Hall of Philosophy was being erected at Harvard, consideration was given to the question of the motto to be placed over the door. The faculty of philosophy proposed the proud statement of the ancient Greeks, "Man is the measure of all things." But President Eliot made the final decision, and these are the words which were carved above the doorway:

> What is man, that thou art mindful of him?
> And the son of man, that thou visitest him?

Thus even in the realms with which science and philosophy deal, there is room for a sense of wonder; and it is, at least in part, out of a realization of the vast mystery by which human life is surrounded that religion itself grows.

If There Were Nothing but Mystery

On the other hand, if there were nothing but mystery there would not be any very good religion. Instead of real religion we would have superstition. The essence of superstition is an unreasoning fear of the unknown. To the superstitious mind the surrounding darkness is inhabited by imaginary terrors. If there were nothing but mystery our religion would probably be a matter of secrecy. As in the ancient mystery religions, the mystery would be revealed only to the initiates. Also the result would probably be sacerdotalism. A certain group of people would claim to have the power to deal with the mystery. It would tell the others that they could not draw near except through the organized group. So, if there were nothing but mystery in our religion, it would not be a very good religion.

Therefore, the real problem is how to have as much of an understanding as we can of the truths of our faith, without losing the sense that there is in them something vaster than we can altogether comprehend. As a matter of fact, in the Bible the word mystery carries the suggestion of both these things. One biblical editor remarks: "A 'mystery' in Scripture is a previously hidden truth, now divinely revealed, but in which a supernatural element still remains despite the revelation."[3] A theologian has written: "Is it not a contradiction in terms to speak of the revelation of something which remains a mystery in its very revelation? It is just this seeming paradox which is asserted by religion and theology. . . . 'Mystery' should not be applied to something which ceases to be a mystery after it has been revealed."[4]

How can we understand the mystery? How can we approach the vastness environing us without forgetting that it transcends our comprehension, yet without falling into an irrational and abject attitude toward it? In what ways can we obtain reasonable intimations of that which in its full scope exceeds the power of human reason to grasp?

UNDERSTANDING THE MYSTERY

One way is by parable. Parables are used many times in the teaching of Jesus. Concerning something that is vast, wonderful, and mysterious, Jesus tells a parable. A parable is literally that which is thrown alongside something else by way of comparison.[5] Thus when Jesus refers to the kingdom of God, he often tells a story which provides an illustration of the meaning which he wishes to convey. Many of these stories were told, on many different occasions. In the Gospels they are at least to some extent grouped together, so they can now be found quickly. For example, in the thirteenth chapter of the Gospel according to Matthew, there are seven parables of the kingdom. Jesus says the kingdom of heaven is like a sower who went out to sow, whose seed fell on different kinds of soil. It may be compared to a man who sowed good seed in his field, but whose enemy sowed weeds among the wheat. It is like the grain of mustard seed, which, though the smallest seed in the world, grows to be a tree. It is like the leaven which a housewife puts in the dough, that the whole may rise. It is like the hidden treasure for which, if you could find it, you would give up everything else. It is like the pearl of great price. It is like the net cast into the sea which sweeps up the good and the bad. These are stories which Jesus told in order to illustrate the great mystery of the kingdom of God.

Or, in the fifteenth chapter of Luke there are three parables on similar subjects. The first is about the lost sheep which the shepherd seeks, though it is only a single animal and far out in the wilderness. The next story is about the lost coin which the frugal housewife sweeps the whole house to find. The third concerns the lost son who is far away from home, for whom the father yearns, and whom the father welcomes when he turns back home again. These are stories which tell us of the love of God for every person.

In other places, too, in the New Testament there are parables and comparisons. Much of The Revelation to John should surely be read in this way. When it speaks about the sea of glass mingled with fire, the streets paved with gold, and the gateways of the holy city which are precious stones, some of the most beautiful things on earth are being used as a comparison for something that is more wonderful than human speech can otherwise express.

Even in our daily experience we may sometimes recognize parables which speak of something vaster. Thus it was with the poet who wrote:

> My faith is all a doubtful thing,
> Wove on a doubtful loom—
> Until there comes, each showery Spring,
> A cherry-tree in bloom;
>
> And Christ, who died upon a tree
> That death had stricken bare,
> Comes beautifully back to me,
> In blossoms everywhere.[6]

Again there is the way of paradox, by which to deal with great mysteries. This is also suggested in the New Testament where in Luke 5:26 the disciples say, "We have seen strange things today." In the Greek it is literally, "We have seen paradoxes today." A paradox is something which is seemingly contradictory, but may yet be true in fact.[7] It is indeed often between the poles of an apparent contradiction that truth is found. The logical position found on one extreme proves unacceptable; that on the other extreme is likewise not to be adopted; thus one is driven to a position in the center between the two, even though the central position appears, superficially, to be logically inconsistent or impossible. This dialectical movement of thought is involved in not a few of the beliefs which have been widely held by Christians.

In one of his books, Donald M. Baillie discusses a number of such doctrines in which the element of paradox is found. For example, Christianity has often taught that God created the world out of nothing, a proposition which on the surface appears incredible. But what are the alternative possibilities? On the one hand it might be said that God made the world out of raw material which was already there, shaping it and manufacturing it, as it were, into what now exists. But this does not represent a very high conception of God, and it makes matter appear godless and inherently evil. That is what we call the dualistic conception. On the other hand is the pantheistic conception. According to this, God created all things out of himself. But that renders creation emanation, a merely verbal concept, making creation merely self-expression. Since neither of the alternative positions is tenable, we are driven back to the teaching which Christian theologians have often enunciated, which at first sounds like an impossibility but now begins to sound like a profound truth, that God made everything out of nothing.

Or consider the doctrine of providence. Here Baillie writes:

> The Christian believes that in some sense everything comes to him *directly* from God, whose working is always individual. And this becomes highly paradoxical when we reflect that in the historical or horizontal network of determinants there are many which are directly contrary to the will of God. The course of my life may be profoundly affected by some injury, which has befallen me through the deliberately evil volition of a fellow man, who seeks to do me harm and is thereby acting directly against God's will. Yet as a Christian I also believe that the thing has come to me from God, who is all-good and all-loving, and who makes all things work together for good to those who love Him. . . . Moreover, however paradoxical this doctrine may be when we try to think it out theologically, the mystery that lies behind it is grasped by countless unsophisticated Christian men and women in the actual life of faith.[8]

Or, as yet another example, take the doctrine of grace. We know that Paul wrote in I Corinthians 15:10, "I worked harder than any of them," and when we remember how far he traveled, how many times he was shipwrecked, and what he went through, we realize that there was a man who put himself into the tasks of his life with the utmost energy and determination. Everything depended upon his own effort. Yet Paul no sooner said, "I worked harder than any of them," than he corrected himself and added, "though it was not I, but the grace of God which is with me." He was doing it all, and yet God was doing it all. In some way those two things go together in the life of a Christian. We have to work as if everything depends upon us, and we have to pray and trust as if everything depends upon God, and only when we hold together the two apparently contradictory sides of the matter do we have the richness of the Christian doctrine of grace.

Thus it is that by the way of paradox we sometimes gain understanding of that which exceeds purely logical comprehension.

In addition to such parables as Jesus gave us, and such paradoxes as are found in Paul's teachings, there is yet another way by which we deal with things which are too vast for the mind wholly to encompass them. This is by knowledge of a person.

When we cannot wholly understand all the profundities with which theology has to do, Christians are still people who believe in Jesus Christ, and believing in him have guidance, light, and leadership. On the level of human relationships, one poet wrote that there were many material things she did not feel sure of or understand but that she had

> . . . certainty enough
> For I am sure of you.*[9]

The poet knew a person, and in spite of uncertainty about many things and the lack of a sure answer to many questions, there was assurance in a personal relationship to a known person. Every person is in some sense a mystery beyond our knowing, yet we do know persons directly and personally. So in Jesus Christ there is mystery beyond our knowing, and yet there is a person whom we know. Christians are people who know him and follow him, and in the knowing of him they have something they are so sure of that they are unperturbed even if they stand on the

* From *Selected Lyrics,* by Amelia Josephine Burr. Copyright 1927 by Doubleday & Company, Inc.

edge of vast mysteries about which they know not yet all the answers. They walk with confidence, though not yet with full knowledge.

In what follows, therefore, we shall think about God, Christ, and the church, using as logical methods of reasoning as we can, yet being willing to heed intimations which may come to us in ways subtler than the reasoning process, and remembering always that our thought will at most comprehend but a small part of what I Timothy 3:16 calls the great mystery of our religion.

PART ONE

GOD

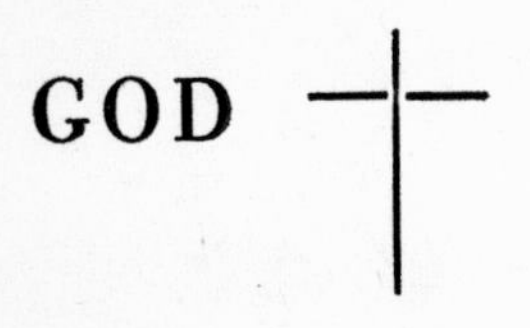

CHAPTER THREE

How Do We Know God?

As we begin our inquiry about God, we may ask what the grounds are upon which our knowledge of him is based?

Our Search

We know God from the fact of our searching for him. Almost everywhere and always, man has sought after God. Prehistoric man buried his dead and indicated his hope for something beyond; he made paintings in the innermost recesses of his caves which suggest that he believed in a power other than himself with which he needed relationship in order to be successful in his struggle for life. From that far-off beginning, through all the stages of human development, man has continued his search for God. The search is well-nigh universal, for there is hardly a people anywhere among whom no vestiges of religion have been found. It is well-nigh unbroken, since it has found expression in every age. Even in those areas of the modern world where denial of God has been a dogma, there is not a little to indicate that belief in him has persisted deep in the lives of a great many of the common people. And it is almost always the case that whatever our sophisticated reasoning, in the great crises of life we cry out for God.

Whether it is in desperate need or wistful longing, men almost always seek after God. Words found in the Maori Poem of Creation have in them something of the feeling of this search: "Seeking, earnestly seeking in the gloom. Searching—yes, on the coast line—on the bounds of night and day; looking into the night." So too does the third verse of Job 23:

> Oh, that I knew where I might find him,
> that I might come even to his seat!

To be sure, the fact that men seek for something does not always prove that it is there. Men have sought for the will-o'-the-wisp, for the pot of gold at the end of the rainbow, and the fountain of everlasting youth, as Ponce de Leon searched for it in the everglades of Florida. Such partial quests, such transitory seekings may not correspond to something that really exists. But this of which we are speaking is something far deeper, more profound, more universal. It is an expression of a religious consciousness which is virtually as ancient and as widespread as man himself. If it is to be compared let it be with some elemental instinct like that which carries the wild fowl across uncharted thousands and thousands of miles to a southern homeland, and leads the poet, seeing the wild fowl winging its way in migration, to speak of the power that will guide his own steps aright. Here is a profoundly deep urge within mankind, and we may believe that it corresponds to something that is profoundly real, that man searches after. Something deep within is turning toward something real without.

It is also true that many who have known this search best have felt that the very fact of man's search for God is in itself a finding of God. Long ago Augustine wrote the well-known words: "Thou hast made us for thyself, and our hearts are restless until they find rest in thee." Thus the very restlessness of man apart from God is itself testimony to God. Amid his troubled search Pascal heard a voice which said: "Thou wouldst not have sought me hadst thou not already found me." This then is a fundamental and undeniable fact, the fact of our searching for God. We know him because we search for him.

His Revelation

We also know God from the facts in which he has revealed himself to us. We, mankind, have been hungry for God—seeking after him through all the centuries. But he has always been active from his side. There are many facts in which he reveals himself to us. All are things for which we are not ourselves responsible. We encounter them. They are given, and in their given-ness is their nature as revelation. There is what God has made. Living in this world, we gradually open our eyes to its wonders and come to recognize the remarkable things that are made—the stars above and the atoms beneath, the sea, the land round about us, the oxygen we breathe, the hydrogen and oxygen that combine to make the water that we drink. We live in the body, and gradually come to realize what an infinitely complex and marvelous mechanism it is, physically. Then we become aware of the directing mind within, and sense the self which expresses itself through mind and body. Then we remember that all this is given to us—man did not make it. Man could not have made it. Man can rearrange existing elements; he cannot create out of nothing. So as we wonder what it means, we arrive at the answer that it is either all just an accident without meaning, or that it is the creation of a Creator.

This much of the knowledge of God, through the things which he has made, has been accessible to all people in all times. Dealing with it is called natural theology. Pagan philosophers as well as Christians have drawn the conclusion of the existence of God from the things he has made. Aristotle, the Greek philosopher, said, that just as in a chorus, when the leader gives the signal to begin, the whole chorus joins in song, mingling in a single studied harmony their varied voices, so too it is with the God that rules the world. He went on to describe the symphony of the world and said that indeed the force that directs it is unseen, but this fact—that it is unseen—stands in the way neither of its action nor of our belief in it, for the spirit of intelligence whereby we live, though invisible, is yet seen in operation.

Seneca, the Roman thinker, stated:

> The eyes of mortals are so sealed by error that they believe this frame of things to be but a fortuitous concourse of atoms, the sport of chance. Yet than this universe could aught be fairer, more carefully adjusted, more consistent in plan? He who . . . established and laid the foundations of the world, who has clothed himself with creation, and is the greater and better part of his work, he is hidden from our eyes. He can be perceived only by thought.

And the Apostle Paul, drawing perhaps upon this very world of Greek philosophy, did not hesitate to declare in Romans 1:20 that the invisible nature of God is clearly perceptible in the visible things which he has made. However, the weakness of this natural theology is patent. As Bishop Aulén has written: "Nature does not under any circumstances give a compelling and unambiguous testimony about the God of faith. . . . The purposefulness of the world is not so conspicuous that it can furnish a self-evident starting point. There is in the world of nature an abundance of phenomena which impress upon us the meaninglessness and the cold insensitivity of existence. These imply a testing rather than a support of faith. . . . Clearly God as 'first cause' has little in common with the God of faith."[1] We must look again.

There is then what God has done. He has not only made this world, he has also worked in it and still is doing so. There has been a slow development of higher forms of life from lower. There has been a tendency, in the long run, for evil arrangements to break down and good to win out. Slavery has been abolished in most of the earth, and colonialism is going today. War has awakened a great revulsion in the hearts of men and a profound longing for peace. The boundless cruelty of Genghis Khan and Tamerlane built nothing permanent. Hitler's thousand-year Reich, founded on racial arrogance and the great lie, fell soon. Communism progresses only by hiding its sinister inner nature and claiming to be the answer to the needs of the common people. On the long-range view, we see evil arrangements breaking down and good winning out.

Or do we? Things appear this way only when, as Reinhold Niebuhr has put it, "the whole human enterprise is seen on a larger stage than the one-dimensional nature-history which the historian's chart shows; for, paradoxically, we detect proofs of the Lord's sovereignty in the whole course of history particularly when we see him making the wrath of men to praise him, and when we see movements not specifically Christian and far beyond the confines of the church, serving providentially to do his will. We then see that his will does not depend on men, that it uses all kinds of instruments for its purpose, including the self-defeat of the sins of men."[2] Then alone do we recognize, as Stephen Neill once remarked, a sort of "grain" to the universe. If you work against the grain of wood it is hard going, but if you work with the grain it goes well. There is a sort of "grain" to the universe: work with it, and things tend to go well; work against it, and they do not go well. G. K. Chesterton once remarked, "Man cannot break the laws of God; he can only break himself against them." Froude, the great historian, said: "In the long run it is well with the good, and in the long run it is ill with the evil."

This is what we mean by saying that God is known to us through what he has done. In thinking this way we are thinking along the lines of the Hebrew people. The Greek philosophers thought in the first way, about what God has made; and they saw him, the invisible, in the visible things that he had made. The Hebrew people had a special sense of God's action in history, and as we read the Old Testament we find a great deal about what God did among men. Learning from that way of thought, we come to recognize him in what he has done and is doing.

Again, we know him from what he has said. As we continue to study the pages of the Old Testament we come upon a whole series of men commonly known as prophets, who stood and affirmed: "Thus says the Lord." Jeremiah was one of these. In one place he declares, "Thus says the Lord who made the earth."[3] So the God who has created all things, speaks. In another passage Jeremiah states, "Thus says the Lord, the God of Israel."[4] Thus the God who was active in the history of the children of Israel, was uttering his word through the prophet. In the case of Jeremiah it is particularly notable that as the message which God gave him to utter, formed itself in his mind, he found it was something which he did not want to have to say. It was harder to say it than not to say it. The speaking of the word of the Lord brought the prophet into trouble. Nevertheless the message burned within him. If he tried to flee from it, it seemed to pursue him. It was like a fire within him until he did say the thing that was given to him to say.

One cannot read about such men as Jeremiah and the other prophets without feeling that what they said truly came to them from without; it was not just something which they made up from their own imagination and desires. Of course it was a message imparted to them within their minds and within their historical situation. But it did not accord with what they wanted to think, or what they would have liked to say. It seemed to come from above, and it was laid upon them with an imperiousness which would not be denied. If then, when we listen to what they tell, something also speaks within us, affirming and confirming the same truth, may we not indeed believe that this is the message of God? Always it is conditioned by the mind of the human being who receives it, and by the concrete historical situation which exists, but it is truly a communication from God. If this is correct, then we know God not only from what he has made and done, but also from what he has said and says.

Once again, we know God from him and through him whom he has sent. In the line of the prophets there came one called Jesus. He was indeed a prophet, as his contemporaries recognized. But one day when he was speaking in the synagogue, he read aloud the words, "He has anointed me to preach good news to the poor."[5] The word "anointed" refers to a specially appointed one. It is the same word as Messiah, and as Christ. Jesus was anointed of God as the Christ to preach the good news to the poor, and when he spoke in the authority of that anointing, he did not express himself as the prophets formerly had done, "Thus says the Lord." He declared: "I say to you."[6] Thus there was a personal embodiment of the thought and message of God in this one, as he brought the good news that the kingdom of God was at hand, and those who were near to him felt near to that reign of God.

These are ways, then, by which we know God. We are engaged in the long search of all mankind, and the very fact of the seeking is in itself in a measure finding. But God is coming to us in what he has made, which we could not make; in what he has done, which accomplishes purposes we may even resist; in what he has said, which comes from without us and speaks within us; and in whom he has sent, the one who speaks with an authority that makes him not just another member of the great universal company of those who seek after God, but also a voice which comes to us from the side of God and with his authority.

He Is

Once again, we also know God from the fact that he is. We know other people from the fact that they are. To know about a person is one thing. That can come from hearsay. It is always something more actually to know that person. When we only know about somebody, we have one kind of knowledge. But when we actually meet him, when we know him personally, that is something else and more. One is haunted, therefore, by the feeling that it may be true that all we have said thus far may have to do with simply knowing about God, and that to know him is something deeper still that can come only from our individual personal encounter with him. Rufus Jones once said that "the theologian seeks for right ideas about God; the worshiper seeks for God himself." Thus it is ultimately the task of theology to lead us beyond theology to worship. That this is possible Augustine assures us when he says: "To arrive where God is, is nothing else but to will to go—to will God entirely is to have him."

So we must continue to think as clearly and consistently as we can about God, that we may have right ideas concerning him; but at the same time we must individually will to meet him if we desire to know him directly, to know that he is already here and just waiting for us to turn to him. Thus we shall not only be a part of the long quest of all mankind, and have eyes open to the facts round about in which God is made known, but we may perchance also know him as one knows a friend.

CHAPTER FOUR

The Nature of God

If we wish to know someone, we naturally seek to learn that person's name. One often goes down the street and hears a little child call, "What's your name?" We do not feel acquainted until we know the name. The Semitic people in particular thought of the name as standing for the character. Thus when it is stated in Revelation 22:4 that "his name shall be on their foreheads," it means that his character will shine in their faces. As a part of our endeavor to understand the nature of God, therefore, we may appropriately ask what names are applied to him in the Bible.

What Is the Name of God?

In the Hebrew language the Bible commonly uses the designation *El* for God. This is the general Semitic term for deity. Suggested derivations indicate that it may have meant Strong One, Leader, or Master. In that case the name of God carried with it, first of all, a sense of awe before overwhelming greatness, yet also a sense of dependence upon one mighty to help. The same word is often found in the plural, *Elohim*. This is probably to be explained as an "abstract plural," a usage which is also found in Babylonian and Egyptian texts, with the meaning "the godhead."

Like the other peoples of the ancient Near East, the ancestors of the Hebrews may at one time have been polytheists. Joshua 24:2 states: "Your fathers lived of old beyond the Euphrates . . . and they served other gods." Then Abraham came to believe in a God who is called El Shaddai.[1] It is thought that this name may be derived from the Babylonian word *shadu,* meaning mountain. As the later Psalmist lifted up his eyes to the hills in quest of help, so this designation would then connect the might of God with the majesty of the mountains. It is not inappropriately translated "God Almighty." Abraham's son Isaac worshiped God under the name of "the Fear of Isaac."[2] His son Jacob reverenced the divine under the designation "the Mighty One of Jacob."[3] Since Isaac spoke of his God as "the God of my father, the God of Abraham,"[4] and since Jacob referred to the one he worshiped as the "God of my father Abraham and God of my father Isaac,"[5] it seems probable that each son had, by deliberate act, chosen as his own the God of his father. Thus the deity could afterward be known as "the God of your fathers, the God of Abraham, the God of Isaac, and the God of Jacob."[6] It is further evident that since the deity had a special relationship to these individual men, their families and their descendants, he was not thought of as limited to some particular place, but was primarily a factor in social and historical relationships. When Abraham left Mesopotamia and went to Palestine it was under the leading of his God. When Jacob went far away from home and at first felt himself to be a wanderer utterly alone, he came to realize that God was even in the desolate place where he pillowed his head upon a stone to sleep by night. Such are glimpses which are meaningful yet today, since we too sing, "Faith of our fathers, living still."

Next, the Bible speaks of God under the name of the Lord. He is not only the God of the fathers, he is also the Lord of the prophets. This new name is introduced at the time when Moses led the children of Israel out of Egypt. Contemplating the hard task of returning from the desert to the land of the Nile and trying to rally the discouraged slaves for deliverance, Moses asked God by what authority he should speak to the Israelites. He was told to say that it was "the Lord, the God of your fathers, the God of Abraham, the God of Isaac, and the God of Jacob,"[7] who sent him. The new name which is used here is spelled in the Hebrew with four consonants: YHWH. When the vowels were supplied in speaking it was probably pronounced something like Yahweh. This name has often been rendered in the English Bible as Jehovah, but is now most often translated Lord. Since God also told Moses to say to the children of Israel that "I Am has sent me to you,"[8] and since there is a Hebrew word *hayah* which means "to be," it seems plainly indicated that this name carries with it the fundamental meanings, "I exist," and "I am present." How appropriate it was that this name of God came into the mind of Moses at that time, may readily be seen. He had to go down to Israel, captive in Egypt, but he could tell them that the One who really is, was with them and was going to help them. God was saying: "I am really and truly here. I am ready to help and to do, as indeed I have always been." What could possibly be more important to these people of Israel than the conviction of the helpful presence of the God of their fathers, with them now, able, mighty, and willing to act? This was what the name conveyed to them, and it was by the same name ever afterward that the prophets most often referred to God. Elijah, discouraged, returned to the mount of God and waited until he heard the still small voice of the Lord. Isaiah and Jeremiah used the name hundreds of times. The Second Isaiah heard a voice which said, "I am the Lord, and there is no other."[9] And we ourselves sing, "Guide me, O thou great Jehovah, pilgrim through this barren land."

Once again the Bible uses the name, "the God and Father of our Lord Jesus Christ."[10] The God of the fathers, who was the companion of the patriarchs, and the Lord who spoke to Moses and the later prophets, became known as the Father. Isaiah 63:16 states: "Thou, O Lord, art our Father, our Redeemer from of old is thy name." Psalm 103:13 declares, "As a father pities his children, so the Lord pities those who fear him." One of the rabbis said: "Be swift as the eagle and brave as the lion to do the will of thy Father who is in heaven." Another asked: "On whom can we stay ourselves?—on our Father in heaven." This usage, relatively scattered and infrequent prior to his time, became the regular way in which Jesus spoke about God. When he taught his disciples a prayer it began: "Our Father who art in heaven."[11] When he himself prayed in Gethsemane he cried to the Father, and at that point Mark preserves the very Aramaic word which he uttered, "Abba."[12] Paul uses the same language when he quotes the customary salutation of early Christian prayer: "Abba! Father!"[13] And we too, likewise taught by Jesus to know the name of God, sing: "Eternal Father, strong to save."

What Is God Like?

We turn next to the question of what God is like, and to this we answer with both negative and affirmative statements. He is not representable by any man-made image. In almost all the other religions of the world it has been felt that God could be represented by such images, but not in Judaism, Christianity, or Muhammadanism. The fundamental commandments of the Jewish faith included a prohibition against the making of any graven image or any likeness of anything that is in heaven or on earth or in the water. On more than one occasion some pagan conqueror of Jerusalem would stride into the holy of holies of the Jewish temple and be amazed to find that it was dark and empty: in it there was no statue to represent God.

God is not picturable as a human being, in a limited, physical form. Some of us naturally enough start out in life with that kind of picture of God. Some of us, then, encounter the modern conception of a vast universe to be measured in light years, and we find difficulty with that early picture. We have concluded, therefore, that we must not think about God as a physical being of limited size and shape, as one would do in a naïve childlike fashion. God cannot rightly be pictured as like that. And yet, as we shall see, we are not forced to think of God as a "vague, oblong blur" (J. B. Phillips) or as a fuzzy part or the whole "of that one shoreless universe which stretches out on all sides to infinity" (Karl Heim). However, God is not fully comprehensible by human thought. Though we shall shortly be making some positive statements about God, we must always remember that our human thought can never fully comprehend him. All that we can say about God will be only a segment of the infinite circle of his reality. We shall be touching only the hem of his garment, as the woman once came and touched only the fringe of the robe of Jesus. "My thoughts are not your thoughts, neither are your ways my ways, says the Lord. For as the heavens are higher than the earth, so are my ways higher than your ways, and my thoughts than your thoughts."[14]

But here, now, are some of the things which on the basis of the Christian faith we may believe that God is, for Christian faith affirms that God was incarnate in Christ and in him reveals his essence and realizes his will. Therefore, we believe that he is personal. The highest thing that we know in the universe is that which is personal. There is the inorganic, then the organic, then the conscious, then the self-conscious, and the whole realm of personality. God, who has made this universe, will not be less and lower than the highest thing that is in it. He will be as high as that, and more. We believe that he is personal because we find ourselves praying to him, and we pray to him because we believe that he is personal. It does not seem reasonable to pray to the law of gravity. You find out how it works, and then try to adjust yourself to it.

God has established laws of the universe, to be sure, and it is highly important to find out how they work, and to adjust ourselves to them, but he himself is more than those laws. You cannot have a personal relationship unless it is two-sided. Between a person and a piece of wood, there is no personal relationship. Between a person and another person there is. We believe that God is personal, and that we have a personal relationship to him.[15]

We believe that God is spiritual. The most important thing about any person is his spirit. This is that which is capable of thinking and willing and loving. The spirit is the incorporeal real self. Here comes death, this strange thing that stills the life of the one we have loved. The body is for the moment just the same as it ever was. Everything is there, except the one thing that really matters—and that is what we call the spirit. So God is the spirit of this vast universe, and is a spirit.

We believe that God is real. At one time men were confident of the truth of materialism. A materialist knew what was real. This table is real because you can feel it; this chair is real because you can touch it; this flower is real because you can smell it; this light is real because you can see it. Of such a materialism we are now somewhat less confident. We are not so sure of the ultimate reality of any of these things which we can see and touch, feel and smell; they have tended to dissolve into something less tangible. A piece of wood or stone or metal is not quite so solid a thing as a materialist used to regard it as being. It is made up, it now appears, of atoms; and these atoms are made up of charges of energy circling in a great emptiness.

These charges of energy can be described only by mathematical formulas. Thus the universe now appears to be fundamentally mathematical, and a mathematical something seems closer if anything to the realm of the mental than to that of the material. It was not inappropriate, therefore, that a physicist made the remark a number of years ago that the universe is beginning to look more like a great thought than like a great machine. Now in such a situation as this, where the material things seem less real than they used to seem, God seems more real because he is the ultimate thinker of the thought that is embodied in what we call material reality. As the thought is more real than the solid substance, so the thinker is more real than the creation. Thus we believe that God is real, and that even if all the material universe should be dissolved and done away with, God would still be.

We believe that God is eternal. How transient everything is, here! Life, after much of it is past, is like a watch in the night when it is over. It is gone swiftly. It is fleeting. The solid world round about—that lasts longer. As we stood upon the edge of the ocean and watched the waves roll in, somebody said, "Think, when this civilization is here no more, these waves will still be rolling in upon this coast." Yes, but even that will change sometime. Even the mountains are wearing down, and presumably this physical universe will some day reach its end. But God, whose world this is, is everlasting. His realm is not limited by time. Time is something that is one of the dimensions of our existence, but his existence is in a dimension where time is no more, and there is eternity.

We believe that God is good. The Bible speaks of

his righteousness and his love. His ways of dealing with us may be ways which are beyond our present knowing, but we believe that the purpose of them is good, and that the long-run, end result of them will be good.

Where Is God?

Yet another question may be asked, and that is, Where is God? To this it may be answered that God is within ourselves. Acts 17:28 quotes Greek poets in the saying, "In him we live and move and have our being." If we live in him, he must live in us. Romans 2:15 declares that God's law is written on the heart and manifest in the conscience of the Gentiles. If, therefore, they would turn within themselves they would find something of God. "Closer is he than breathing, and nearer than hands and feet," writes the Western poet. "Manifest, near, moving in the cave of the heart, is the great Being," declares the Eastern sage. It is within, that God is felt as a presence, heard as a still small voice, and encountered as a structure of values.

He is also within our neighbor. The commandment to love your neighbor as yourself is stated to be "like"[16] the commandment to love God, that is, it is of equal weight and importance. "He who does not love his brother whom he has seen, cannot love God whom he has not seen," is the conclusion of I John 4:20. God must, in some sense, be in one's neighbor.

God is everywhere. He is in heaven but also in Sheol, and not even in the uttermost parts of the sea is man absent from him. His worship can be limited neither to Mount Gerizim nor to Jerusalem, but as a

Spirit he is to be worshiped everywhere in spirit and in truth. So it is that a contemporary Christian poet has written:

I am not alone
By night,
Or by day,
Or by circumstance;
Neither in the silence,
Nor in the city's roar;
Nor as I lie
At the door of death,
Or stand on the
Threshold
Of a new life;
For thou art with me—
Around me,
Underneath me,
Bearing me up,
Giving me strength,
Luring me on.

I am not alone;
Thou hast been,
Thou wilt be,
Thou art
With me.
Lo, I am always in Thy care. *Amen.*[17]

CHAPTER FIVE

God and Nature

The next step in our investigation is to discuss more fully the relationship of God to the world of nature. We shall begin where mankind began, as nearly as we can tell, in thought about this matter, namely with the prescientific view of nature.

The Prescientific View

Primitive man saw nature as pervaded by mysterious force or animated by living spirits. To these views we give the names of dynamism and animism. Exposed as he was to hazards of accident and disease, and placed as he was amidst the perils of wild beasts, flooding rivers, and flashing lightning, primitive man must have been much afraid. In happenings hostile to himself he must have read an unfriendly intention, and in those which benefited him he may have felt a friendly purpose. Thus much of his life must have been overshadowed by dread of the potencies of nature; yet he may have been drawn, too, to the worship of these forces in awe and gratitude. In general, therefore, he seems to have believed that there was power or that there were spirits in nature.

Early civilized man also experienced what he interpreted as an encounter with personal wills in the realm of nature. As an expression of this understanding he formulated myths. Expression of such myth-producing thought may be studied in the extensive literature of ancient Babylonia. For example, where we would explain that atmospheric changes had taken place to break a drought and bring rain, the Babylonians related that the great bird Imdugud had covered the sky with the dark storm clouds of its wings and devoured the Bull of Heaven, the hot breath of whose nostrils had been withering the crops. In similar fashion, the Egyptians told how it was that the sun, which was believed to have been the first king of Egypt, was now in the sky. Becoming weary of close association with humanity, the sun-god Re took his seat upon the sky-goddess Nut. She then assumed the form of a huge cow standing over the earth. Thus it came to pass that the sun has its place in the sky.

The witchcraft of preliterate man, as found for example among the Azande of Africa, also involves belief in mysterious and sinister forces operative in the world of nature. A Zande boy strikes his foot against a small stump of wood in his path in the bush. The wound becomes infected and causes much pain. He would not dispute the fact that the stump of wood had grown naturally in the path. But he would feel that the facts that he struck the stump even though he was walking as carefully as ever, and that the wound festered instead of healing quickly as is usually the case, were proof that witchcraft had been practiced against him. Thus in the realm of nature there are not only natural happenings but there is also an interplay of more mysterious forces of the sort with which witch doctors have to do.

On the whole, then, the prescientific view saw divine and demonic powers in nature, and led man to an attitude of either dread or worship with regard to the forces and spirits which were believed to be in the objects of nature.

The Scientific View

With advancing knowledge, the belief that there were spirits inhabiting the objects of nature came to appear superstitious. Emancipation from this belief was brought by the development of science. What we recognize as the scientific spirit is clearly found among the Ionian Greeks of the sixth century B.C. Settled in Miletus and other cities on the coast of Asia Minor, these Greeks numbered outstanding thinkers in their midst. No longer responding to the objects of nature with either dread or worship, they sought to find some underlying principle in all the phenomena of the natural world. Thales, a mathematician, thought that everything was made out of water. Anaximander, a geographer, spoke of the "boundless" from which all things came. Anaximenes, a pupil of the latter, held that everything was made of air, in varying degrees of density. Following these pioneers, later Greek philosophers enunciated ideas which sound very much like theories current in modern science. Practically anticipating the theory of evolution, Heraclitus declared that all things change. Speaking like a nuclear physicist, Democritus stated that all things are composed of atoms.

In this way of looking at nature there seems to be no necessity of saying anything about God. It is sufficient to find out how nature operates and deal with it accordingly. Since this can be done without making any mention of God, God appears to be irrelevant and is even held by some to be nonexistent. Man has not only been delivered from superstitious fear or abject worship of the objects of nature: he has been left in a natural world with which God seems to have no necessary connection.

Much scientific thought has been characterized by materialism. This is the doctrine that things are made of matter, that matter is what you can know by your senses, and that matter is what is real. Thus anything which cannot be apprehended by sight, touch, or other senses, appears to be unreal or at least seems to be unimportant.

Scientific thought has also been marked by determinism. Matter behaves dependably. Given the same conditions, you will have the same happenings. Drop an object, and it will always fall to the ground. Add two units of hydrogen to one of oxygen, and you will always get H_2O and it will be water. If you knew all the conditions you could obtain all desired results. That Thales predicted an eclipse in 585 B.C. was a direct result of his method and a proof of its effectiveness.

Furthermore, the thought of science has included the conception of coincidence. The way in which things fit together to affect man is the result of the interlocking of separate patterns of events. In so far as these patterns are out of man's control, their impact on him may be in terms of accident, chance, and mischance.

According to the scientific view as held by many people, therefore, nature can be described and dealt with without any reference to God. If mythological thought was typical of much of the ancient world, this scientific thought has been characteristic of a great deal of the modern world.

The Biblical View

Turning now to the biblical view of the relationship of God and nature, and in the light of what has been said already, we are immediately struck by the fact that biblical religion was just as effective in emancipating man from dread or worship of nature as was Greek science. In the experience of Elijah, recorded in the nineteenth chapter of I Kings, God was not in the wind or earthquake or fire. In the eighth Psalm it is said that the heavens are the work of his fingers and that the moon and the stars were established by him. In the nineteenth Psalm it is stated that the heavens declare the glory of God. In the fortieth chapter of Isaiah, God is described as spreading out the heavens like a tent, and man is urged to lift up his eyes on high and see the whole host of heaven which God numbers and calls by name. In Matthew 5:35 heaven is called the throne of God, and earth his footstool. From the point of view represented in these and many other biblical statements, there is no slightest thought of worshiping the sun as the ancient Egyptians did, or fearing the storm clouds as being demonic spirits or mysterious divine power. The God of the Bible is lifted high above nature, and all the objects of nature are things which God has made. It is right, therefore, neither to worship nor to fear the objects of nature, but only to worship and to fear the exalted and infinite God. But God's glory is shown in these things, and he, the Creator of all, must never be forgotten.

How thoroughly and radically this biblical view did emancipate the Hebrews from the prescientific thought of Mesopotamia and Egypt has been set forth in a book on *The Intellectual Adventure of Ancient Man,* written by a group of scholars of the Oriental Institute of the University of Chicago. In it, William A. Irwin states that "the boundary between the ancient world and the modern is to be traced, not in the Aegean or the middle Mediterranean, but in the pages of the Old Testament,"[1] and H. and H. A. Frankfort write:

> When we read in Psalm 19 that "the heavens declare the glory of God; and the firmament sheweth his handiwork," we hear a voice which mocks the beliefs of Egyptians and Babylonians. The heavens, which were to the psalmist but a witness of God's greatness, were to the Mesopotamians the very majesty of godhead, the highest ruler, Anu. To the Egyptians the heavens signified the mystery of the divine mother through whom man was reborn. In Egypt and Mesopotamia the divine was comprehended as immanent: the gods were in nature. The Egyptians saw in the sun all that a man may know of the Creator; the Mesopotamians viewed the sun as the god Shamash, the guarantor of justice. But to the psalmist the sun was God's devoted servant who "is as a bridegroom coming out of his chamber, and rejoiceth as a strong man to run a race." The God of the psalmists and the prophets was not in nature. He transcended nature—and transcended, likewise, the realm of mythopoeic

thought. It would seem that the Hebrews, no less than the Greeks, broke with the mode of speculation which had prevailed up to their time.[2]

But biblical religion not only agreed with Greek science in delivering man's thought from bondage to fear or worship of the objects of nature: it also preserved and emphasized certain aspects of the understanding of the relationship of God and nature which have tended to disappear from purely scientific thought. Instead of glorifying nature as the only reality, it has kept nature as God's handiwork. It is a great and infinite God whose thought is expressed in the world of nature, whose power is over it and whose wisdom is in it.

Thus we have a view which transcends the materialism often characteristic of science. In a materialistic philosophy, what matters is matter, and nothing else is real. On such a theory, mind itself becomes an enigma. How has it ever happened that we have the power of thought, that we are conscious of ourselves, and that we wish to find truth and have beauty and accomplish goodness? How could atoms, ricocheting in accidental fortuity, ever arrive at such results? Actually, in our day, matter does not look as solid as it used to look, and mind and matter are recognized as having effective interrelationships. Even the existence of the soul seems not only an intuition of selfhood but also a hypothesis necessitated by the actual facts of personal transcendence of space and time. According to the biblical view, God has made all of this, this world of matter, this world of mind, and this world of spirit.

Whereas scientific thought alone has often been

deterministic, by the biblical view we can declare that neither man nor God is imprisoned within a deterministic scheme. Man must be free at least within limits, because the Bible is all the time saying, "Do this. This thou shalt not do." It brings its exhortations and commandments, and these make sense only if we have freedom to do or not to do. And God must be unlimitedly free, bound only by his nature, by goodness and love. If man is free within limits to use the patterns of nature to accomplish his ends, much more God must be free to work in this great pattern of nature which he has made toward the purposes which are his infinite and ultimate will.

Once again, whereas science has only been able to speak of coincidence when things fit together with peculiar and particular meaning for an individual person, by biblical faith we are taught that in its inner meaning the fitting together of things is itself within the providence of God, and that to those who love him all things work together for good.

God then, by biblical understanding, is infinitely above the world of nature, so one need not worship the objects of nature, nor dread them either. One is free to study them, as the scientist does, and the words of Jesus promise that the knowledge of the truth will lead to greater freedom. But above the world of nature, and expressed in it, are the wisdom and the greatness of God. It is his glory which is manifested by his heavens, and all his handiwork.

CHAPTER SIX

God and Man

Since we have set forth in some detail in the preceding chapter how the biblical view of God and nature compares with prescientific and scientific views on the same subject, now as we consider the relationship of God and man, we may proceed directly to a systematic statement of biblical teaching on this subject.

Creator

The Bible says that God is the creator. There are many places where it refers to his work of creation, and five places where it uses the title "Creator" for him. "Remember also your Creator in the days of your youth." "The Lord is the everlasting God, the Creator of the ends of the earth." "I am the Lord, your Holy One, the Creator of Israel, your King." "They served the creature rather than the Creator." "Let those who suffer . . . entrust their souls to a faithful Creator."[1]

As the creator, God made man in his own image. This is stated in Genesis 1:27: "So God created man in his own image." And it is said in Genesis 2:7: "Then the Lord God formed man of dust from the ground, and breathed into his nostrils the breath of life." To say that God made man out of the dust of the ground means, as we would put it, that God made man out of the fundamental elements of the universe. Man is made out of atoms and molecules just like everything else in the universe. As the astronomer Edwin B. Frost once somewhere wrote:

> We are such stuff as stars are made of. The elements that make up our bodies are the most common elements on the earth, and our telescopes reveal nothing in the farthest star that isn't found on our own planet. . . . We see that we belong to a going concern, and no amount of thinking about the vastness of the universe and the smallness of man can overwhelm us when we remember that we are star dust. We are samples of the Creator's whole universe. We are citizens of the cosmos, incomprehensibly huge as it is.

To say that God breathed into man the breath of life is to say that God gave man his spiritual nature. Breath is the symbol of life and of the soul. In the thought of primitive men everywhere it has been natural to identify this intangible vapor which we call breath, which goes out of a man when he dies, with the very life or soul. Therefore the early writer of the second chapter of Genesis is doubtless explaining that God who made man out of the common elements of the universe, also put into him something of his own life, his own soul, and his own spiritual nature. That is why we can say that God made man in his own image, because he gave him a nature with spiritual qualities that are like unto the spiritual qualities of his own nature, while, at the same time, maintaining the radical discontinuity between himself and man. For, after all, the essential being of man and God are not the same; not "of the same stuff" nor "of one piece."

Between this biblical account of the creation of man and the account provided by modern science, there is no necessary contradiction, provided only that we recognize here in the Bible a story written in what we would call poetic and symbolic terms and find in the work of science a prose narrative, as it were, worked out by patient, empirical induction. The one in poetry and the other in prose tell us a common story. It is a fact that we are here on a planet where there is a range of temperature that is just that in which life can exist, where there is a combination of chemical elements that gives us water to drink and oxygen to breathe, and the other necessary provisions to sustain life; and that here on this planet life has actually come up from simple beginnings to more and more complex forms and to higher levels of consciousness, self-consciousness, and awareness of spiritual values where we think of truth and beauty and goodness and where we know hope and faith and love. This, which is indubitable fact, seems in full agreement with what the Bible states as fact, namely that God has made man in his own image.

But the Bible also indicates that God made man free. Continuing the biblical story about these early beginnings, we find that the first man and the first woman were put in a beautiful garden, as their place to live. They were shown all the trees, many with fruits, round about, and were told that of all of them they might freely eat, but of one in particular they might not eat. That is exactly, in a poetic story of early beginnings, a description of man's freedom. He knows within himself that there are many things which he may rightly do, and some things that he should not do, but he is left free to make the final choice himself. Why does that commend itself to us as indeed the truth about man? Because it feels that way to be alive. It feels as if we have some choices to make when we live. Of course, we realize that heredity conditions our life. Of course we realize that environment makes a difference. But we see some people who have a fine heredity and a favorable environment who make a mess of things. We see some others whose backgrounds have not been too good, and whose surroundings have not been too fortunate, who rise magnificently above it.

So we realize that in the last analysis the outcome of life depends upon the choices which the individual person makes. Indeed, God could hardly have made man in any other way than this and still have made him in his own image. Here is a piece of inert matter: it has to obey the laws of the physical universe. Here is a growing plant: it goes through a process of development, but without its own volition. Here are living animals: they live and move and act rather freely, but seem to be guided largely by what we call instinct. Perhaps that is why they do not get into as much trouble as we, because for the most part they follow the unerring guidance of these patterns of behavior that have been built up over so long a time. But no one of these is a full image of God. It is only man to whom God gave the gift of freedom, and it is only man who is described as being made in the image of God.

Now when God made man in his own image and made him free, he also took a risk. He took a risk of ruin, and set up at the same time the possibility of progress. To turn the kind of being who was man loose in the world was a risk. There was the risk that man being free in the world would burn down the forests with his carelessness, would slay the animals with cruel wantonness, would fight against his fellows with more and more terrible wars, would fill himself full of drugs and drink until he behaved worse than the self-respecting animals, and would forget his Maker. On the other hand, there was the possibility of progress. There was the possibility that man would become a partner with God in what God wished to accomplish in this universe. Professor William E. Hocking once wrote a book with the striking title, *What Man Can Make of Man.*[2] There is the possibility of the making and remaking of man, until his nature should reach what God wanted it to be. But that could come about only if man, being free, wished to co-operate with God and God's purpose.

JUDGE

The next thing that the Bible says about God in relation to man is that God is the judge. Many biblical passages speak of God as the judge. "Shall not the Judge of all the earth do right?" "The Lord is a God of knowledge, and by him actions are weighed." "God is a righteous judge." "He comes to judge the earth. He will judge the world with righteousness, and the peoples with his truth." "But you have come . . . to a judge who is God of all . . ., for our God is a consuming fire."[3]

Many things in life make us realize that God is a judge. God has put a moral law above us. The great philosopher Immanuel Kant said that two thoughts overwhelmed him and filled his soul with wonder. One was the thought of the starry heavens above, and the other the thought of the moral order. The moral order is as much above us as the starry heavens. When man acts as if he were superior to the moral law it is disastrous. Of course it is true that there is a development in the understanding of the demands of the moral order, but there is still something absolute about it. As the philosopher, A. C. Garnett, has pointed out, there is an absolute in ethics. It is the Golden Rule which is stated in some form or other in at least ten great religions of the world. It is the demand that we should do good to others, equally with ourselves. This law is over us; God has set it in the structure of things, much as he has set the laws of physics in the structure of physical things. It cannot be gotten away from. It cannot be broken. You can break yourself but not the moral order.

Then God has put a conscience within us. This is something in ourselves which tends to swing into line with the moral structure of the world. Of course, even a conscience can get out of order; it can stand in need of education, can need repairing and getting straightened out. Some time ago a round-the-world steamship was several hours late in departing through the Golden Gate. The captain had halted the ship in the middle of the bay, and was swinging it to the different cardinal points in order to calibrate the compass. It was necessary to have it in good working order before they got out on the boundless sea where there were no longer any fixed landmarks by which to check their direction. We need that sometimes. That is no doubt part of what church and church school are for, to help us get our conscience lined up with the everlasting principles of God. But God the Creator gave us something within us that tends to swing in that direction.

One more thing shows us that God is truly the Judge, and that is that we do encounter judgment here and now as well as at the end of the road. The desolation and alienation, the continued bondage to self, that come when God's will is not being realized, when we oppose him, may be said to be his judgment. At the end of every road there is a judgment. What we did, and what we did not do comes home to us. If that happens already here and now in life, there is little doubt that it will happen in a climactic way at the end of life. Then all that we have been and done will be summed up and laid bare in the presence of God. So it is that the Bible speaks of God as judge.

Redeemer

But once more in relationship to man, the Bible teaches that God is redeemer. "O Lord, my rock and my redeemer." "Your redeemer is the Holy One of Israel." "Thou, O Lord, art our Father, our Redeemer from of old is thy name."[4] This tells us that God is really concerned with us. He really cares about us and wants to help us. If he were only Creator, making this world and leaving it as it is, if he were only Judge, causing these inexorable laws to work out to their inexorable end, then this might not be so. But he is more than that, he is also Redeemer. He has made us and wants to bring us to what his purpose is for us. He does judge us, because his nature is righteous, but he redeems us because his nature is love.

As redeemer, God suffers for us. Here are a few sentences from a recent book in the field of theology:

> To say that God suffers means that he is actively engaged in dealing with a history that is real to him. What happens makes a difference to him. . . . The world's sorrow and agony are real for God. . . . Suffering is the way love wins. . . . A father does suffer with his son. How much more, then, does God's love achieve its deepest meeting with us, and its ultimate victory through God's suffering. He is not all suffering. He is power. He is inexhaustible creative energy. To say that God suffers does not take away from the majesty or the power of his love. It is rather the proof that his love has a strategy for dealing with evil.[5]

God the redeemer forgives. Here is a sentence from Howard Thurman's *Meditations of the Heart.* "Self-examination issues most often in a sense of sin, the acknowledgment of which is the first step in the forgiveness of God."[6] Think how remarkable that is. The acknowledgment of sin ought to put us in a place where God the judge would be able to condemn us. But it is when we acknowledge our sin that we have taken the first step toward the forgiveness of God. Christianity's even deeper insight is that we are able to acknowledge our sins only through the grace and help of God, so that truly God takes the initiative. This supplants the Jewish notion that man makes the first move—an offering, an acknowledgment—and then God accepts. This view affirms that nothing done by self-effort is a requisite for winning his forgiveness. It comes through his initiative and self-sacrifice. "If we confess our sins, he is faithful and just, and will forgive our sins and cleanse us from all unrighteousness."[7]

As the redeemer, it is the purpose of God to bring to glory his children, "for the creation itself will be set free from its bondage to decay and obtain the glorious liberty of the children of God."[8]

A traveler, recently returned from Africa, told this story about a new Christian convert. Until a very few years ago the man had been a cannibal. When the missionaries told him that God was the creator, he said readily that he understood that. He pointed to the trees and said, "The trees grow." And though he had doubtless never heard our poem, he said, "Only God can make a tree." This he understood. Then the missionaries told him that God was the judge. He also comprehended that idea quite readily, and said, "I understand that if you want to get a magnolia tree you do not plant a mahogany tree. You get the result of what you do. I understand that God is the judge." Then they tried to tell him that God is the redeemer. That was harder. It was several days before he came back. Then he said, "Yes, I understand that too. The Arab slave traders used to go into the jungles and take our people captive. They would put great iron collars around their necks and lead them away. Sometimes the chief would see one of his friends in that group of slaves, being led away. He would go to the Arabs and say that he would give so much ivory, so much gold to set that man free. The trader would take the ivory and gold, then go to that man and remove the great rough iron collar from his neck and set him free. I understand that God loved us enough to do everything so that we might be set free, so that the iron collar of sin and ignorance, of superstition and disease might be lifted from our shoulders. I understand that God is the redeemer."

Such, by the teaching of the Bible, is God our Creator, our Judge, and our Redeemer.

CHAPTER SEVEN

God and the Realm of Accident

We live in a world which we believe was made by God and is ruled by God. We also live in a world in which there are accidents. Accident, by the very etymology of the word, means something which falls upon or befalls one; an undesigned and unexpected event; an occurrence, particularly one that is of a harmful sort, and unforeseen. What is the relationship between God and accident?

The Ancient Theological Answer

The ancient theological answer to this problem no longer seems wholly satisfactory. This answer is that God sends accidents to punish sinners; therefore if a person suffers an accident, you may be sure he is a sinner. There are many places where this has been shown to be unsatisfactory. In the Old Testament there was the case of Job. Job was a good man. He had seven sons and three daughters. The oldest son celebrated a birthday. The other children came to his home for the celebration. While they were enjoying the birthday dinner a great wind came across the wilderness, struck the house, and killed all the young people. This and many other accidents befell Job. His friends, using the old theological theory, told him he was clearly a sinner. He knew he was innocent. And the rest of the book is taken up with wrestling with that problem. A man who has not committed a great sin, for which these would be the proper punishments, nevertheless experiences these terrible blows.

In the teaching of Jesus the ancient theological answer is shown to be unsatisfactory. Referring to the eighteen whom the tower in Siloam fell upon and killed, he asked, "Do you think that they were worse offenders than all the others who dwelt in Jerusalem? I tell you, No."[1] The Siloam tower may have been a part of the fortification of Jerusalem, in the vicinity of the well-known pool of Siloam. Presumably it was built of great stones. But it must have had a poor foundation, or it had been weakened by earthquakes; at any rate the stones had begun to shift, one upon the other. The tower still looked just the same as always, but actually it was in a state of delicate equipoise. At the very moment when these eighteen people were standing in the shadow of it, the stones came loose, crashed down and killed the eighteen. Why? The popular answer was that the eighteen were sinners. God caused them to be there at the time that the tower fell. Jesus said flatly that this was not so.

Yet another place where the old answer has been shown to be unsatisfactory is in Thornton Wilder's *The Bridge of San Luis Rey*. This, it will be remembered, is the story of a bridge across a chasm, which falls when a certain five persons are on it. The problem is why that particular group of five was on that bridge at the moment when it went down. Brother Juniper was interested in this problem, and felt that by showing an exact equivalence between punishment and character he could demonstrate the fact of God and God's justice. When the pestilence visited his village of Puerto, it seemed like an opportunity to study the matter on a scientific basis. He secretly made a tabulation of the characteristics of fifteen people who perished in the pestilence, and of fifteen people who survived. But the results were perplexing, because those who perished turned out to have been five times more worth saving than those who survived. And the people on the bridge were not all bad or all good, but such a strange mixture that it was difficult to equate what happened to them with the justice of God working out in such an accident. In these and other places, then, the ancient theological answer to the problem of accidents has been shown to be an unsatisfactory one.

A New Answer

Next we shall ask whether from science and religion together, it is possible to frame a more satisfactory answer about the relationship of God and accident. When we spoke about God and nature in general, we observed that the prescientific view saw animating spirits and dynamic forces in the objects of nature. Then Greek thought began to study nature for itself, and so set us on the way to science. But also it let some of us feel that it was not necessary to talk about God at all any more. Biblical and Christian thought also set us free from worshiping and dreading objects of nature, and therefore equally left us free to be scientists, but also taught us that the world of nature is God's creation and that he rules over it. So there ought to be some way to put together, in a modern view, science and religion in relation to our problem.

Let us come at it first, then, from the side of science. Science tells us something like this about accident: We live in a dependable world of cause-effect sequences. Accidents are explainable in terms of cause and effect. We have, for example, the law of gravitation as formulated by Newton. This states that any two material bodies, if free to move, will be accelerated toward each other with a force proportional to the product of the masses of the two bodies and inversely proportional to the square of the distance between them. This turned out to be not a completely accurate description, and Einstein refined it, and said something like this: Moving bodies follow the shortest tracks in space-time. These tracks are curved toward massive bodies, and smaller moving bodies appear to be pulled down toward them. Now the practical application of this is that if a man is on the roof and becomes free to move because his shoes slip, the smaller body, which is he, is accelerated toward the larger body, which is the earth, with destructive force upon impact. This is a scientific description of the accident in terms of the law of gravitation.

Or, take the law of centrifugal force, which refers to the kind of force which flings something outward around a center of rotation. The law is: centrifugal force equals $\frac{mv^2}{r}$. M is mass, v is velocity, and r is the radius of rotation. You can tell at once upon looking at that formula, what is going to happen. V is velocity. You increase your velocity, and note in the formula that the v is squared, so a small increase in velocity results in a squared increase in force. The r is underneath the line, which means you divide by it. Thus the smaller the radius is, the greater your force becomes. Now suppose you do both those things at the same time when you are driving around a corner. You increase your velocity, and this increase is automatically squared; you shorten your radius which is the dividing factor, and the result is a great increase in centrifugal force. The result is also that your automobile goes over the curve on the corner. That is a scientific explanation of an automobile accident.

The point of the scientific view is, thus, that accidents are describable by known formulas; they are not random happenings, and they are not to be attributed to God. Fundamentally they are due to ignorance when we do not know what the relevant laws are; to carelessness when we know the laws but do not obey them; and to irresponsibility when we act without proper regard for others who may be harmed along with or even instead of ourselves. The application of this scientific view to the problem of accidents is very constructive and very helpful. For example, drivers in high school training courses and professional drivers under training have recently been reported as having an accident rate of 1.96 per hundred thousand miles, whereas the rate for ordinary drivers is 3.45. Therefore, we can get at the problem of accident constructively and helpfully from the scientific angle.

Now let us come in from the other side, that of

religion. What does Christian faith in God have to do with the problem of accidents? For one thing, as has already been implied, Christian faith in God helps us to be free from the old superstitions, so that we may freely learn and know the laws of the universe and adjust our lives to them. In the old days when men were afraid of evil spirits, when they felt themselves subject to blind fate, there was no encouragement to try to learn the laws of nature and adjust life to them. Actually the biblical faith has been one of the main things that liberated men from that old bondage to the spirits and fate, and set them free to think and to learn. Any individual scientist may or may not think that he needs Christianity to help him to learn about the universe, but historically Christianity has actually done a great deal to set men's minds free from the blanket of superstition and the curse of fatalism so that they can learn these things.

Furthermore, our biblical and Christian faith puts us upon a way of life that saves from, and in, accident. The following writer appears to believe that all accidents are pure coincidences; in other words he takes a point of view which would commonly be recognized as completely scientific. He simply regards accidents as coincidental, some being fortunate and some unfortunate. But when he asks what our faith has to do with it he makes this very important suggestion:

> If we love and serve God . . . we shall be saved from a number of unfortunate coincidences. We shall not be caught cheating in an examination, as were some well-known College football stars recently. If we love God, we shall strive to take good care of our bodies and minds because they are dedicated to his purposes. Therefore, for instance, we shall not be the cause of

automobile accidents, as will those who have little regard for themselves or their fellows. If we love God with alert minds as well as affectionate hearts, we shall have courage, wisdom and strength in meeting a critical situation or emergency which may save our lives and others. Love for God will save us *from* some unfortunate coincidences and *in* some unfortunate coincidences.[2]

Can we get any farther than that? May it be that faith in God and life in full dependence upon his providence give to man a sort of radarlike guidance through the space-time tracks of the world? A psychologist has noted two strange but complementary series of facts. On the one hand, if a person becomes disintegrated in himself and his personal relationships, then, in too many cases to be dismissed as coincidental, he seems to attract to himself an unduly large proportion of untoward events. On the other hand, the highly integrated seem to attract to themselves an unduly large number of favorable events, which work to forward their progress.

Following this clue, another writer dares to suggest that anyone whose will is wholly united with God is delivered from accident. This does not mean, I think, that what a scientist would describe as an accident would not still happen, but it does mean that even it would be within the providence of God and all its terror would be removed. Here is the illustration which the writer proposes: A man is going up the mountainside. An avalanche is coming down the mountainside. The avalanche is following its track in space and in time. It is a minute phenomenon which accompanies the contraction of the surface of the earth, and is perfectly definite, perfectly describable.

The man coming up the mountain is also following his own track in space and in time. But he is a man whose mind is with God, and as far as his mind is raised to God he is aware of this minute, rigid, future event that is about to take place. His conscious mind need not know it, but a leading can make him go faster, change his route, or wait. Or, it may make him go straight along to be overwhelmed in the avalanche. But for that, too, he is equally ready, knowing intuitively that the time has come for his body to be disposed of. Thus there is and can be no accident, though to others it will seem so, because this man is ready with a fully creative response and acceptance. Thus to the man who wholly dwells in God there is never anything to fear.[3]

Deeper Meanings

Whatever theoretical understanding of the entire problem one may find convincing, it certainly belongs to the Christian faith to point us to deeper meanings in accidents which do transpire. We are all in a world that is full of forces more vast than we, and our lives are subject to the impact of untoward events of which our conscious minds, at least, have no advance inkling. When unfortunate circumstances befall, we all need practical help. One of the suggestions which the Bible makes is that an accident may be a warning. This seems to be the meaning of the statement of Jesus about the eighteen persons upon whom the Siloam tower fell. They were no worse sinners than anybody else, he said, "but," he added to those who were listening, "unless you repent you will all likewise perish." An accident may be a call to return to God. It may be a warning that we are allowing disintegration to take place within ourselves, our minds, our spiritual nature, our relationships to other people. When an accident does occur, much depends upon the spiritual state of the one who experiences it. Persons who are right with God, with their fellows, and with themselves, may handle it magnificently. But if we are wrong with God, with other people, and with ourselves, then when an accident strikes us, conscience brings with it its own condemnation. Then the outward blow becomes far more shattering and is far more difficult to overcome. So accidents can be a warning.

Accident again can be a testing. That is the way it is described in the Book of Job in relation to that man. His ill fortunes were a test which was allowed. God does allow us to be in this kind of world, where he has not set up absolute safeguards all around. If he has allowed this kind of existence, then perhaps he is testing us in it. Parents let a little child try to toddle across the floor, even though it may take a tumble and receive a bruise; that is a necessary part of growth. Perhaps the hard experiences of life are a necessary part of the growth of character, and a testing of character. A few years ago a high school girl was swimming in Lake Tahoe when a speedboat swept across her and she suffered the loss of both feet. In a San Francisco hospital I saw her in a wheel chair, cheering up another girl younger than herself. Not long ago, she walked across the platform of her high school and received her diploma. She said to those who inquired about her future plans that she was intending next to go to college to learn physical therapy. "I want," she said, "to work eventually in veterans' hospitals teaching the disabled how to walk again. I think it is my place to give them the benefit of my experience." She certainly stood that test magnificently.

Once again, accidents may be a blessing. This blessing may be so deeply hidden that only faith can even dimly discern it, yet perchance it may be a fact. In the summer of 1953 a group of American climbers were only a few thousand feet short of the summit of K2, the second highest mountain in the world. A terrific storm pinned them to their high camp. One man, Art Gilkey, fell ill with thrombophlebitis, and blood clots formed in his lungs. Though the storm was still raging they started down to try to get him off the mountain. At one point they stopped to reconnoiter the further way and fastened the sick man on his stretcher firmly to a great bank of snow. They suffered a slip—five men fell hundreds of feet and were arrested by the belay of one man. Eventually they climbed back up to where Art had been left. In the meantime an avalanche had swept him away completely. One of the members of the party afterward wrote that at that moment the death of Art seemed the ultimate cruelty of fate, yet that the ways of providence are inscrutable and that perhaps it was for the best. It seems apparent that the others never could have carried their crippled companion off K2 alive. Why the rest of them came through unharmed, they do not entirely know. The mountain was terrible, "but," said the writer, "a higher power may have been watching over."

We remember that as the story of *The Bridge of San Luis Rey* is brought to its conclusion, the reader is left with the feeling that some merciful divine motive may have been at work even in that tragedy. If one knew all, much would be clearer; perhaps everything would be explained. The last sentence in the book declares that between the land of the living and the land of the dead, the bridge is love. So to live in love of God and our fellows will bring meaning even in accident.

CHAPTER EIGHT

God and Evil

In the discussion of the problem of evil it is customary to distinguish three different kinds of evil.

WHAT IS EVIL?

The first kind is the evil of imperfection. Philosophers often use the word "evil" with this connotation. They refer to the necessary imperfection of the creature as compared with the creator. The creator we think of as perfect; we as creatures are imperfect. There is an incompleteness, a lack of wholeness, which belongs to all created things. We sometimes speak about "this present evil age," and imply that the perfect age and the perfect world lie in the future. When we think about ourselves we feel that we are imperfect, we sense imperfection in ourselves and recognize imperfection in the things that we do and make. We do the best we can, yet the best we can do is not so good as we wish it might be. If we do the worst we can, what we do is certainly terrible, but even when we make our very best effort, what we accomplish always in some way falls short, and we have to try again. There is, therefore, a way to do something about this kind of evil that is imperfection. We are all engaged in the struggle against imperfection when we seek to do a better piece of work, speak a better word, write a better sentence, or attain a higher goal. This kind of evil is the resistance against which we strengthen the muscles of our endeavor.

Then there is the evil of accident. This was considered in the preceding chapter, where it was recognized that in the realm of accident there are both fortunate and unfortunate happenings. Thus not everything about accidents is evil. And even in regard to the unfortunate eventualities there are ways in which we are saved from them and saved in them. There is the way of science through which we trace out causes and effects, and by eliminating certain causes reduce disastrous happenings. There is the way of theology through which we penetrate to deeper meanings of that which befalls, and are able to find positive good beneath the negative surface of some events. In so far, also, as evil befallings come in the train of moral wickedness they will have some mention in the present chapter.

Thus it is not the evil of imperfection or the evil of accident in which we find our hardest problem. Imperfection necessarily inheres in creation, because it is essentially an ongoing process, incomplete in any particular moment; accident seems inevitable in a world of causes and effects. But there is yet another kind of evil, and it is in it that we confront the deepest difficulty. This is the evil of moral wickedness. Men know what is good and choose to do what is bad.

Men experience the bitter contradiction within themselves which Paul described so vividly when he said that the good that he would he did not, and the evil that he would not, he did. In the Old Testament the Hebrew word for evil is *ra.* In many passages such as the following it is clear that it connotes moral wickedness: "You have sold yourself to do what is evil in the sight of the Lord." "You love evil more than good." "Their feet run to evil."[1] The corresponding word in the Greek New Testament is *poneros,* and we find it also many times: "The bad tree bears evil fruit." "The evil man out of his evil treasure brings forth evil." "Hate what is evil." "Abstain from every form of evil."[2] When we study the use of these two words we also notice that they are frequently used to refer to calamity. They connote adversity, affliction, distress, grief, misery, sorrow, trouble, wretchedness, harm, and hurt. It is suggested therefore, that moral wickedness often brings calamity in its train. Thus the Bible gives us a picture of the kind of evil which is moral wickedness, and which is followed in many cases by calamity and trouble.

Whence Comes Evil?

It now becomes necessary to ask whence evil comes. Does evil come from God? Did God create the evil of moral wickedness? In the sixth and seventh verses of the forty-fifth chapter of Isaiah there is a statement which appears to answer these questions in the affirmative. The prophet reports God's word as follows, according to the King James Version: "I am the Lord, and there is none else. I form the light, and create darkness: I make peace and create evil." In order to assess this verse fairly we must remember the situation the prophet confronted. He faced the existence of idolatrous polytheism all about him; people believed in many different gods, and represented them in various images. He refers to that in the twentieth verse of the same chapter where he says, "They carry about their wooden idols." Over against that situation the prophet is saying that there are not the many different gods portrayed in these many different idols; there is just one God, who has created everything that there is.

But the prophet probably also had to face the challenge of Persian dualism. The forty-fifth chapter of Isaiah is addressed to Cyrus, the king of Persia. At that time or before that time Zoroaster had preached in Persia. His teaching was that the world is in two parts evenly balanced against each other, one part darkness, one part light, one part evil, one part good; in the world are two primal spirits, one the spirit of good, the other aligned against him, the spirit of evil. Our biblical prophet, therefore, may be understood as saying that even that is not the case, that there is just one God, the creator of everything. There are not two gods fighting with each other in this world, but one who is so supreme, so infinite, so exalted, that everything is his handiwork. From that angle, then, the prophet made the otherwise rather surprising statement that the one God has made the darkness as well as the light, and has created evil as well as peace. This writer did not want his people falling into what the Persians believed, that darkness was just as strong as light and evil was just as much a force as good in the world. Rather, he declares, there is just one great God over everything.

Since we also believe in this fundamental proposition of the unique sovereignty of God, do we also have to think that God has created evil? In the two following ways we can give an affirmative answer to this question. First, God made man able to choose wickedness when he made him able to choose goodness. But what alternative would there be? Only that God should make man like a robot, an automaton. Intricate and amazing machines are being made these days, and they do remarkable things, but you know one thing, and that is that they never do anything except what they are set up to do, and they will never make any response except according to the stimuli which are provided for them. It will be a predetermined response. God could have made man like that, but then where would the glory be? It would be gone, because man would respond automatically every time. Sometimes we wish it had been that way, for it would be easier if all our responses were controlled automatically. But the glory of a free choice of the hard right against the easy wrong would then not exist.

The glory of all the deeds of heroism and self-sacrifice which men have done would not be. Recently a jet airplane being flown by a test pilot experienced a "flame-out." The pilot could doubtless have saved himself by parachute. But he was over a heavily settled area at the time, and to have abandoned the plane would have endangered lives below. So he stayed in the cockpit and fought desperately with the controls of the almost unmanageable machine until he "pancaked" into a swamp at over 300 miles per hour, himself suffering severe injuries. This was the heroic deed of a free man. There would be no glory if there were no freedom. So when God made man able to choose goodness, he had to make him able to choose badness and evil. In that sense God did so arrange the world that there is evil in it.

In the second place, God created evil in the sense that he made the kind of world where calamity follows sin. We have already seen how the biblical words for evil contain the two meanings of moral wickedness, that is, wrong choice, and calamity. Sorrow and wretchedness are sure fruits of sin. It is thus correct to translate Isaiah 45:7 as is done in the Revised Standard Version: "I create woe." The evil which God has made is the woe, calamity, and disaster which follow upon evil choice. He has made the kind of world in which these are consequences of wrongdoing. How could he have made any other?

Still pursuing the inquiry as to the source of evil, we may now ask the further question as to whether it comes from Satan? At this point, perhaps, what we should really ask is, "Where does Satan come from?" It seems definitely possible that the conception of Satan came from Persia where, as we saw, there was a dualistic framework of thought and a belief in two opposing forces. On the one hand was Ahura Mazda, the god of light; on the other, Angra Mainyu, the demon of darkness. It is a fact that the doctrine of Satan does not attain prominence until in the later books of the Bible which for the most part are believed to have been written after the Jews had dwelt in Babylonia and been under Persian influence, or at least in a position to be influenced by Persian thinking. So there is a very real likelihood that the idea of Satan came from Persian influence. It is there, certainly, in late Judaism. In the time of Jesus there was common belief in the devil and in many demons who went about doing what the devil wanted them to do. Finally, as is shown in Revelation 20:2, the identification was made of Satan and the devil with the ancient serpent which had tempted Eve as narrated in the book of Genesis. Thus when the great early prophets of the Old Testament were coming to the fundamental understanding of the one God of the world, they did not speak about Satan. The conception of Satan is relatively late, and may have come in from Persia. Jesus used it as he talked, just as he accepted in general the way people did speak and believe in his day and spoke in the same way, but we are not necessarily required to have as an item in our creed, "I believe in Satan." As a matter of fact, the very careful biblical scholar Alfred E. Garvie said plainly of the whole body of ancient demonology: "Christian faith need not burden itself with this load of Jewish beliefs."[3]

But now, lest by tracing historical origins we too readily dismiss significant ideas, let us not fail to recognize that there are many circumstances in life where we act as if Satan were setting his hand upon us. "He is possessed," we say. "What got into that person?" we ask. "What got into me? How could I have done what I did?" I have heard a psychologist speak about "autonomous complexes originating in and arising out of the subconscious," as being exactly what they called being possessed by a demon in New Testament times. Prior to World War II men spoke of how the nations were moving against their will toward some terrible catastrophe, as if a sinister force were driving them to do what they would not do. There are experiences in individual life and in the social order where it seems as if a power were getting hold of us which is more than we are, and which drives us toward things which in our best natures we do not desire. So, as a tentative conclusion we may hold that Satan is a personification of these forces in the universe. Nevertheless it may seem more probable to some that these forces are actually the manifestation of a personal demonic will and that Satan is an actual person. It must assuredly be admitted that there are many verses in the later parts of the Bible which speak as if this were the case.

Evil, then, comes because God has made a world where we are free to choose goodness, therefore can choose badness. And the evil of calamity comes because the world is a moral order where sin is followed many times by disaster. There are also forces that seem to be more than ourselves within ourselves, and within our society, which drive us to things of which we are afterward horribly ashamed. These forces even seem to have a sort of entity in themselves outside of ourselves.

But finally evil comes from man himself. God has made a world which could still be "very good," as he himself is said to have called it at the beginning.[4] But from the very outset, things have gone wrong where man was concerned. Now so many wrong things have been done all together, that the weight of them has piled up cumulatively and all mankind bears a burden of evil. But it is still most of all the result of the fact that man himself has chosen wrong when he could have chosen to do something right.

Perhaps the supplication in the Lord's prayer, "lead us not into temptation,"[5] still sounds as if the ultimate responsibility were upon God rather than man. I think, however, that this means we are asking God please to lead us, and may it not be into temptation. Even in the early church there may have been misinterpretations of this supplication, and James 1:13-15 sounds as if it were written to guard against this danger: "Let no one say when he is tempted, 'I am tempted by God'; for God cannot be tempted with evil and he himself tempts no one; but each person is tempted when he is lured and enticed by his own desire. Then desire when it has conceived gives birth to sin; and sin when it is full-grown brings forth death." Such is the teaching of the New Testament on the question we have been discussing.

What Is God Doing About It?

When we ask what God is doing about the evil of moral wickedness we find that the Bible is full of teachings concerning redemption. The Old Testament declares the unique sovereignty of God, and tells of his moral governance of the world, describes the evil imaginations of the heart of man, and narrates the disasters which came upon man for his wrongdoing, but it does not stop there. It also contains in many forms the promise which is stated in the following words in II Chronicles 7:14: "If my people who are called by my name humble themselves, and pray and seek my face, and turn from their wicked ways, then I will hear from heaven, and will forgive their sin and heal their land." Furthermore, the New Testament tells about the Son of man who "came to seek and to save the lost," states that "the blood of Jesus his Son cleanses us from all sin," and conveys the assurance that there is "now no condemnation for those who are in Christ Jesus."[6] There is, therefore, an answer which God has provided for the problem of evil, and it is specially connected with Jesus Christ. Christ will accordingly be the theme of the next section of this book.

evil ways; then I will hear from heaven, and will forgive their sin and heal their land." Furthermore, the Second Testament tells about the Son of man who came to seek and to save the lost," states that "the blood of Jesus his Son cleanseth us from all sin" and conveys the assurance that there is "now no condemnation for those who are in Christ Jesus." There is therefore an answer which God has provided for the problem of evil, and it is specially connected with Jesus Christ. This will accordingly be the theme of the next section of this book.

PART TWO

CHRIST

CHAPTER NINE

God Was in Christ

God, of whom we have been speaking in the preceding section of this book, is declared in the New Testament to have been in Jesus Christ. A concise affirmation of this fact is found in II Corinthians 5:19, where Paul states, "God was in Christ."

At the Height of Human Development

In the endeavor to understand this fact we may think of Jesus Christ as standing at the height of human development. At another point in his correspondence with the Corinthians, Paul makes a reference which suggests this line of thought. In I Corinthians 15:45 he compares and contrasts Christ as the second Adam, with the first man, the first Adam. So the first man, Adam, was the beginning of human development. If we were to give a description of the beginning of the life of mankind on earth as we know about it through scientific investigation, at the present state of study, we would say something like this: The first manlike creatures probably appeared upon earth far back in the Pleistocene epoch, say five hundred thousand years ago. As the great family of mankind came on the scene it is technically designated as the genus *homo,* using the Latin word for "man." One of the best-known representatives of early mankind is Neanderthal man, so called because his skeletal remains were first found in the Neander valley in Germany. This man dates back perhaps one hundred thousand years ago. He was heavily built, had a low broad skull and a brain as large as that of modern man. He lived by hunting, used flint tools, and buried his dead. Then came *homo sapiens,* "man the wise," the same species which inhabits the earth today. He is well known from discoveries at a place called Cro-Magnon in France and elsewhere, and he probably lived some fifty thousand years ago. Cro-Magnon man is distinguished for his intellectual activity as revealed particularly by the magnificent mural paintings which he put in the innermost chambers of the great caves of Europe. Such were some of the beginnings of human life on earth as far as we know it from science today.

Between what has just been told and what is narrated in the Bible there is no necessary contradiction. What the Bible gives is a poetic and symbolic account of the origin of man. In Genesis 2:7, which is quoted in part by Paul in I Corinthians 15:45, it is stated that "the Lord God formed man of dust from the ground, and breathed into his nostrils the breath of life, and man became a living being." This states, as we would put it, that man was made out of the fundamental elements of the universe. If we were to write it today in terms of chemistry, we would say man is made of carbon, of which the symbol is C, phosphorus, P, magnesium, Mg, iron, Fe, and sulphur, S. These elements of course are made up of atoms, and they in turn of protons and electrons.

Proud as we are of our ability to turn the poetic statement of Genesis into the precision of a chemical formula, we should not forget that if we were to write that formula—namely, CPMgFeS—on the blackboard, we would not be able to recognize our best friend in it. There is something about man besides that which is described in the chemical formula. That is the other part of what Genesis says, "God breathed into his nostrils the breath of life, and man became a living being." Man's self-conscious life is a mysterious gift to him from God.

Justification for the interpretation I have given of the Genesis account is found, it seems to me, in the fact that this poetic writer gives to the first man the name of Adam, which is simply the Hebrew word meaning "man." Like the scientist in his different fashion, this writer, too, in his own symbolic way was telling about the origin of man. Scientific research can show us something of the long process through which God worked. The book of Genesis can remind us that in addition to the dust of the earth out of which man was made, he was given a spirit that came to him from God.

That was the beginning of human development according to science and the Bible. Since the point we wish to make is that Jesus Christ stands at the height of human development, we must say something as to what this development consists in. It was a physical evolution. Man stood up on his two feet, and attaining an erect posture, was able to see farther and have his hands set free. No longer like the creatures that must use all four feet to walk on, man could employ his hands for profitable work. Also, the hand of man is marvelously contrived, so that thumb and forefinger are opposed, and he can pick up tiny objects and do delicate things. Such, fundamentally, was man even in Neanderthal and Cro-Magnon times, and such is he today. Indeed he still has left over, it seems, a few items like the appendix which are of no apparent value any more, but which witness to the earlier stages from which he has progressed.

Then there is mental development. Already Cro-Magnon man, who made the marvelous paintings that still adorn the walls of his prehistoric caverns, seems to have been mentally, as well as physically, much like man today. Vast accumulations of knowledge have of course been built up since that time, but in essential ability Cro-Magnon man must have been well equipped.

Further, there is social development. This involves learning how to live with other people—something that modern man himself does not seem to know very well how to do even yet. Both in personal social relationships and in international relationships he is constantly involved in difficulty.

Finally there is spiritual development. The physical development is in relationship to physical environment—material things. The mental development is in relationship to mental environment—ideas, meaning. The social evolution is in relation to social environment—other people, either individually or in larger groups. The spiritual development must therefore be in relation to the spiritual environment, and that is in relation to God. Here we have presumably only barely begun. We have made but the beginnings of learning to live in harmony with God, of knowing the vastness of his power and experiencing the reality of his guidance. Progress here would seem to belong to the future of man's development. When asked what would happen in the next fifty years, Dr. Charles Steinmetz once said: "I think the greatest discoveries will be made along spiritual lines." "Some day," he continued, "people will learn that material things do not bring happiness and are of little use in making men and women creative and powerful. Then the scientists of the world will turn their laboratories over to the study of God and prayer and the spiritual forces, which as yet have been hardly scratched. When that day comes the world will see more advancement in one generation than it has seen in the last four."

What we are now saying is that Jesus Christ stands already at the height of human development. He represents these last steps and stages. To have performed the labors and endured the sufferings which he did, he must have been a person of physical strength. He undoubtedly had great mental power, as was evidenced in his handling of the Scriptures and his discussions with other people. More than that he represented right life in social relations, and the kind of attitude toward others which, if followed by all, would bring happiness and welfare to all. Most of all he represented the true and right spiritual life, the kind of relationship to God and the spiritual realities of the universe that gave him unprecedented power even in mental and physical realms, and that was manifest in the yet more important realms of love and goodness among people. God made Adam the first man and made him a living being. He made Christ the second man, the second Adam, and made him, as Paul called him, a life-giving spirit.

It is here claimed, therefore, that there is something new in Jesus Christ. At each stage along the way of human evolution there has indeed been something new. First came matter, then life. Who would have dreamed, seeing inert matter, that there would ever be life? Who would have dreamed, seeing the early protoplasmic beginnings of life itself, that man would come? Who would have foreseen that in man, thought, conscience, and faith would emerge? At each one of these steps up along the line something happened that was surprising, unexpected, and unpredictable. Something took place at each point which cannot be explained as adaptation to environment, for adaptation to environment would work for equilibrium. Were that the whole principle of evolution, then some sandworm or other primitive form of life which has attained perfect adaptation to environment, and has not changed in a million years, would be the chief result. Instead of that has come change, novelty, and surprise. Along this line, Lecomte du Noüy suggested some years ago in his book on *Human Destiny* a hypothesis of telefinality, as he called it, which supposes that there is a force at work which orients the entire march of evolution and has acted, ever since life appeared on earth, as a directing influence tending to develop a being endowed with a conscience, and made morally and spiritually perfect. It is in harmony with this suggestion to regard Jesus Christ as the already present, and indeed ageless, example of that spiritually perfect man of the future. He stands at the height of human development.

At the Depth of Divine Condescension

We may also think of Jesus Christ as standing at the point where God reaches down into human life. There are several places where the Bible has something to say about this side of the matter. One is in the record of the birth of Christ. The genealogy of Jesus as found in the third chapter of the Gospel according to Luke, states that Jesus Christ was the son, as was supposed, of Joseph. Joseph was the son of Heli, he was the son of Matthat, and so the line goes on back to David, to Abraham, and finally to Adam, who was, it is said, the son of God. Now if that first man who was the beginning of human development upon earth was the son of God, how much more so was this last man, this second Adam, who is the height of that development, in whom not only the physical and the mental but also the social and the spiritual have reached their climax? Shall we not indeed call him the Son of God? So the Bible proceeds and tells about the wonderful fact of the birth of Christ. George A. Buttrick comments on the narrative: "There is a mystery in Christ which human factors alone cannot possibly explain."[1]

Then the Bible tells about his baptism, and states that when Jesus was baptized, being about thirty years of age, a voice came from heaven saying, "Thou art my beloved Son; with thee I am well pleased."[2] This evidently means that Jesus had so lived during the first thirty years of his life, that God spoke to him at that time as his own well-pleasing Son, and gave him special work to do.

When the New Testament tells about the resurrection of Christ, it not only affirms that he was "descended from David according to the flesh," which is the side of the matter of which we were speaking before, but also says that he was "designated Son of God in power according to the Spirit of holiness by his resurrection from the dead."[3] That is the other side. God reaches down and exalts him in the resurrection. Jesus was a man physically descended from David and Adam, but when he showed himself so faithful to God that he even died on the cross, God raised him from the dead and declared to everyone that he was his Son.

Once more the New Testament states that Jesus Christ is the word of God. "In the beginning was the Word . . . and the Word became flesh and dwelt among us."[4] A word is first of all an idea in the mind and then it is an expression of that idea which communicates it to others. Thus, to say that Jesus Christ is the Word of God is to signify that he is God's thought, and also the expression of that thought in human life. A translation of the passage in the Fourth Gospel to which we have just referred, which was made in one of our colleges, gives this meaning very well:

> In the beginning was the Idea, and the Idea was with God, and the Idea was divine. All things were made in pursuance of that Idea and without it nothing was made. The Idea was the sustaining Substance, the Inner Reality of all that was made.
>
> The Idea became alive and the Life of it was the Light of men, the true Light that lighteth every man that cometh into the world. The Idea was made flesh and dwelt among us full of

grace and truth. No man hath seen God at any time, but no man having once seen that Life full of grace and truth can fail to catch the Idea.[5]

Such are some of the ways in which the Bible speaks about God as coming down in the life of Christ. He stands at the height of human development, but also at the depth of God's condescension to our earth.

At the Point of Personal Encounter

Once again, we may speak of Jesus Christ as the one in whom we experience an encounter with the divine. According to a story found in the fifth chapter of the Gospel according to Luke, Peter was once out fishing. After a fruitless night, Jesus told him where to cast his nets, and this time the nets came up full. When Peter saw what happened, he fell down at Jesus' feet and cried, "Depart from me, for I am a sinful man, O Lord."[6] Later, after the disciples had time to know him longer, Jesus asked them what others thought about him, and then what they themselves thought about him. This time Peter said, "You are the Christ, the Son of the living God."[7] Yet again, after Peter had failed wretchedly and denied Jesus three times over, he met the risen Christ at the Galilean lake. As narrated in John 21, the Lord asked Peter three times over if he loved him. And Peter, speaking contritely, humbly, and with a greater depth of sincerity than ever before, said thrice over to Jesus, "Lord, you know that I love you." Peter's experience is our experience. Meeting with Christ, we meet one who makes us aware of our sinful selves; one who elicits from us confession of personal faith; one to whom we wish to say, coming back after any failure, "Yes, Lord, you know that we love you."

So it is that as Carl Knudsen somewhere has written: "The fact remains that men who were closest to Christ were compelled to come to the conclusion that in him they saw the face of God shine through upon men."

CHAPTER TEN

The Only Son

When the New Testament speaks about Jesus Christ as the Son of God one fact which is brought into view is that of his solidarity with all mankind.

Solidarity

In the preceding chapter attention was called to the genealogy in the third chapter of the Gospel according to Luke, where the ancestry of Jesus is traced all the way back to Adam and God. Jesus was the son of Adam, who was the son of God. If we seek to follow the line of descent in the other direction, we find the book of Genesis telling how God made Adam, the first man, out of the dust of the ground and breathed into him the breath of life. The son of Adam was Seth, his son was Enosh, and the further descendants were Kenan, Mahalalel, Jared, Enoch, Methuselah, Lamech, and Noah. Noah had three sons, Shem, Ham, and Japheth. In the tenth chapter of Genesis these three are pictured as the ancestors of the three great branches of mankind. The sons of Japheth are the people known as Indo-Europeans; the sons of Ham are the Africans; the sons of Shem are the Semites. The branching families of earth, Semites, Indo-Europeans, and Africans, are all children of God, for all are descended from Adam, God's son. Thus it is the teaching of the Bible that all people upon earth are children of God. Individual persons therefore are sons of God. Some of us may be lost sons, some of us may be prodigal sons, but by the word of the Bible, all are sons.

Accordingly, when the Bible speaks of Jesus as the Son, it justifies our emphasizing his solidarity with all men. The Letter to the Hebrews also says this explicitly, and declares that "he had to be made like his brethren in every respect."[1] Jesus Christ, the Son of God, was made like his brethren in respect of suffering. "Although he was a Son, he learned obedience through what he suffered," says Hebrews.[2] He was made like men. In his suffering he was betrayed, taken captive, and tried. Yes, he suffered more than most. He was mocked, scourged, and crucified. The way upon which he walked with his last steps upon earth has since been called the Via Dolorosa—the way of sorrows. The cross, which was the instrument with which the Romans executed their worst criminals, has ever since been remembered as his sign. Suffering people, ever since, have felt a kinship with him. The innocent man unjustly accused, the weary burdened down with toil, those sick and in pain, all have felt this relationship, for he was made like unto them and unto us in respect of suffering.

He was the Son, and was made like unto his brethren in respect of human feeling and emotion. As we read the Gospels we are told that he was fatigued: "Jesus, wearied as he was with his journey, sat down beside the well."[3] He experienced hunger and thirst. He knew grief: "Jesus wept."[4] He knew wrath: "He looked around at them with anger."[5] He, the Son, was made like unto his brethren with respect to the facts of his space- and time-conditioned existence. He lived in Palestine, a diminutive land, and hardly ever went outside its boundaries. He lived as one of the Jewish people, in blood and culture and in religion. He went to the places to which they went to worship, the synagogue and the temple. He used what they used for Scriptures, what we call the Old Testament. He observed the Passover. He lived in what we today would call the prescientific age, and spoke within the framework of first-century beliefs about the structure of the universe, the prevalence of demons, and the end of the age. Henry J. Cadbury once wrote a book on *The Peril of Modernizing Jesus,* which pointed out that in our studies we are in danger of making him like somebody of today and forgetting that he really lived there and then. Jesus actually lived as a real person of that time and place. So he was made like unto his brethren, in every respect, and when we speak of the Son we speak of one who is one with his brethren.

Pre-eminence

But the Bible not only speaks about Jesus Christ as the Son of God, it also speaks of him as the first-born son. Paul uses this language in Romans 8:29 when he concludes a sentence about Jesus as the Son with the statement "that he might be the first-born among many brethren." This suggests and justifies our laying emphasis upon his pre-eminence. He is the first among many brethren. When the Jewish people spoke about the first-born it meant a great deal to them. The first-born in the flock belonged to God, and the first-born son received a double share of the inheritance. When God says in Exodus 4:22 that "Israel is my first-born son," witness is given to the pre-eminence of the people of Israel in God's plan. When it is said in Psalm 89:26-27 that the king will cry to God, "thou art my Father," and that God "will make him the first-born," the pre-eminence of the ruler is recognized. Therefore when Christ is spoken of as the first-born Son, testimony is given to his pre-eminence among all.

Jesus Christ was the first Son to have everything in subjection under him. Hebrews 2:8 quotes Psalm 8:6 in an interesting way. The Psalm speaks about man and says, "When I look at thy heavens . . . what is man that thou art mindful of him?" Then it goes on, "Thou hast made him little less than God . . . thou hast put all things under his feet." As the author of Hebrews thinks about that passage and quotes it, he says, "We do not yet see everything in subjection to him." Man is not yet in the position of having everything in subjection to himself. "But we see Jesus," continues the same writer. Thus it is intimated that the glorious position which God intended for all men has actually been occupied by Jesus.

He was the first Son to attain full spiritual stature. The goal for all, according to Ephesians 4:13, is to come "to mature manhood, to the measure of the stature of the fullness of Christ." This means that he already has that spiritual stature which it is God's desire and purpose that men should come to have. He is the first Son to have been raised from the dead and manifested to men in full glory. When Paul declares in I Corinthians 15:20 that "Christ has been raised from the dead," he also continues, saying that he is "the first fruits of those who have fallen asleep." Just as in the other examples we have given where that which is purposed for men is already realized in Christ, so here. In him first, in us later. That which is planned for God's other children is already actual in him. In the history of religion we find stories of Baal and Osiris and others who were slain and who came back to life again. But those are mythological figures, and the stories about them are expressions of the hopes and desires of men. In the Gospels there are accounts of how Jesus brought Lazarus and the widow's son back to life. But whether it was from death or seeming death that he brought them back, they were only restored for further life for a while longer upon this earth. In the records of spiritualistic experience are the testimonies of those who claim to have been in touch with the departed. But the evidence is scattering and often tinged with uncertainty. Never has there been such a full and convincing manifestation of the resurrection as in Jesus Christ. When he was raised from the dead and manifested to men in the glory of his spiritual existence, it was a happening which the disciples found utterly unprecedented. So he is the first-born, the first Son to be raised and made manifest to men in the gloriousness of his resurrection.

Uniqueness

There is yet another way in which the New Testament speaks of Jesus Christ. He is called not only the Son, and the first-born Son, but also the only Son or the only begotten Son. The Greek word applied to Jesus in John 3:16, translated "only begotten" in the King James Version, and "only" in the Revised Standard Version, means that he is unique, the only one of his kind.[6] Jesus Christ was the only Son who did not sin. He was tempted in every respect as we are.[7] That was involved in his solidarity with mankind. But he did not fall in sin. "Which of you convicts me of sin?"[8] he asked of the men of his time. This was a bold thing to say if there were some sin hidden away there that might be pointed out and brought to light to his condemnation. But in his life there was no sin, and nothing to be concealed. It was not that he was unable to sin, but that he was able not to sin. Among all mankind he is the only Son in this respect. Even in the Muhammadan religion Jesus is pointed to as the only sinless one.[9] The Qur'ān of course makes the claim that Jesus has been superseded by Muhammad, but when it speaks of the one who was without sin among men, it is to Jesus that it points.

He is also the only Son who fully knew the Father. He again spoke a word of great audacity but also of simple truth when he said, "No one knows the Father except the Son."[10] Therefore he is likewise the only Son who gives us a wholly satisfying representation of God. "He who has seen me," it is written in the Fourth Gospel, "has seen the Father."[11]

"If Jesus was not a unique revelation of God," wrote Christian F. Reisner, "then we have no more concrete picture of God than has any other religion. . . . Some minds cannot grasp the idea of an invisible God; such folks are greatly helped by comprehending a manward expression in the historical Christ. Unless God is as personal as we are, then it is impossible genuinely to worship him or hope to come into contact with him. . . . It is possible to imagine Jesus as a personality lifted until he is infinite. That fits the Christian conception of Christ."[12]

CHAPTER ELEVEN

Christ and the Other Religions

According to the New Testament teachings which we have been studying, the Christian religion believes that God was in Christ, and that he was the only Son. But there are other religions in the world. What about them?

A Traditional View

A view which has long been held on this subject may be stated something like this: "Christ has the truth. The other religions are false. Therefore they should be displaced and destroyed." There may seem to be support for this attitude in the statement of Jesus that "he who is not with me is against me."[1] Ancient Christian theologians maintained this position. They held that God founded the Christian religion, but Satan founded the other faiths. E. D. Soper remarks that "this was a simple solution of a difficult problem, and it carried the Christian Church until within the last century or two."[2] Likewise the relatively recent book by Hendrik Kraemer on *The Christian Message in a Non-Christian World* holds that biblical realism requires an attitude of "intrepidity" toward the non-Christian religions.[3]

We may agree with this intransigent view to the following extent: There are false and wrong things in many religions of the world. There is much superstition. Superstition is an unreasoning fear of the unknown. It is an irrational, abject attitude of the mind, and it includes all the things that men do because of this fear and this unreasoning attitude. Here is a child in Singapore. It cowers in fear as an eclipse of the sun takes place, because it has been taught that there is a dragon up in the sky which is devouring the sun, and it is afraid. Here is a native in Sumatra. He is wasting away and dying. His enemy has hired a magician. This man of magic has made a little clay image to represent the man and has set the clay statuette at the edge of the river. The water of the river is lapping against the clay statue and is washing it away. As it disintegrates, this native weakens, and as the last of the clay disappears in the stream, he dies—of fear.

There is idolatry among many of the religions of the world. Idolatry is the worship of a physical object as a god. We go into a museum and see tiny statues and great images, often grotesque, often with exaggerated features, which are idols. But when we go around the world, we find these figures still set up in shrines and temples in many places. Priests wash and clothe these idols, worshipers bedeck them with flowers, give them food, and spatter upon them the blood of sacrificial animals. Reginald Heber had not yet gone to India when he wrote, "From Greenland's Icy Mountains," but after he became Bishop of Calcutta he had abundant opportunity to see what he had already written about in that hymn in the words: "The heathen in his blindness bows down to wood and stone."

There is polytheism among many religions in the world. This is belief in numerous gods. The sun, moon, stars, mountains, rivers, and other objects are all deities. Different aspects of life have gods and goddesses presiding over them, such as education, harvest, fertility, fortune, and so on. With polytheism there is a scattering of loyalty and an ultimate uncertainty as to whether the right god is being worshiped.

There are personality-destroying philosophies in some of the religions of the world. The doctrine of transmigration and reincarnation under the inexorable law of Karma, for example, teaches that the nature of your present existence is due to your deeds and misdeeds in previous lives, and there is nothing you can do about your present situation except to endure it, in the hope that when you die and are born again it may be on a little higher level and in a little more fortunate circumstance. The fact that this doctrine is taught most vigorously by those who are themselves at the top of the present system of society and obviously desire to stay there, makes one doubtful of it, and makes one feel justified in saying that this has worked against rather than for the development of individual personality.

There are society-retarding practices in some of the religions of the world. In so far as caste is a form of societal organization which is sanctioned by religion, and which restricts you in your occupation and your opportunity to the position and place into which you happen to be born, so that there is nothing you can do about it, it seems to be a system which hampers rather than releases the fullest energies of the members of the social order.

At all these points there is in Christ truth which is opposed to these false and wrong things, truth which ought to have a chance to displace and overcome them, and to bring light where there is darkness. From this point of view we can join Reginald Heber in singing:

> From Greenland's icy mountains,
> From India's coral strand,
> Where Afric's sunny fountains
> Roll down their golden sand,
> From many an ancient river,
> From many a palmy plain,
> They call us to deliver
> Their land from error's chain.

A Modern View

Next we must consider another view of the relationship of Christ and the other religions. It is one which has been widely held in modern times, and it runs somewhat like this: "Christ has truth. The other religions have truth. Therefore we should keep the religion we already have and let the other people keep theirs. Or at most we might think of mixing them generally together at some time in the future." For this attitude there is some support in the statement of Jesus that "he that is not against us is for us"[4]; and in the affirmation of Hebrews that God has spoken in many and various ways by the prophets.[5] Surely God has not left himself without witness anywhere.

There are true and fine things in the other religions

of the world. There is belief in one God in many other places of the world. In the mosques of Islam is inscribed the verse of the throne, as it is called. It goes like this:

> There is no god but he, the Living, the Eternal; slumber affects him not nor sleep; to him belongs whatever is in the heavens and whatever is in the earth . . . his throne extendeth over the heavens and the earth, to guard them wearieth him not; he is the Exalted, the Mighty.

Such a passage might be read alongside some of the Psalms of the Old Testament. Most of the sayings in the Qur'ān begin with the statement: "In the name of the merciful and compassionate God." That is the kind of God we believe in, one marked by mercy and compassion. Everyday Hinduism means bowing down to wood and stone, but an emancipated educated Hindu philosopher speaks very differently. Swami Nikhilananda, for example, says that the oneness of the Godhead is a chief doctrine of Hinduism. It is because the Godhead is unknown and unknowable, he explains, that Hindus use various symbols through which to contemplate it.

The Golden Rule is taught in other religions as well as in Christianity. In one form or another it appears in almost all the advanced faiths, from the saying of Buddhism, "Hurt not others with that which pains yourself," to the teaching of Zoroastrianism, "that nature only is good when it shall not do unto another what is not good for its own self." Fundamentally they are all trying to say the same thing at this point, and I would be only a hopeless bigot if I should declare that all those other formulations mean nothing, and only mine means anything.

There is also saintly character among the adherents of other religions of the world. Gandhi of India was called Mahatma, which means "great soul," and we can hardly deny that the appellation was fitting. Nevertheless Gandhi always remained a Hindu, and in the last week of his life testified to his devotion to that religion and spoke of himself as a reverencer of the cow. Today one of Gandhi's spiritual heirs is Vinoba Bhave. Though he is old and ill, he is walking across India, through the villages, asking rich and poor alike to give away one-sixth of their land, so that the ten million families in India who own no land whatsoever may have some. One must surely recognize the saintliness of such characters, even though they belong to other faiths.

In Christ there is a spirit which does recognize this and does rejoice in it. If Reginald Heber could pen "From Greenland's Icy Mountains," another great follower of Christ, George Matheson, was able to write:

> Gather us in: we worship only Thee;
> In varied names we stretch a common hand;
> In diverse forms a common soul we see;
> In many ships we seek one spirit-land.

A Comprehensive View

Now we confront a dilemma. The traditional view points out properly enough that there are false and harmful things in the other religions, and these should be displaced and destroyed. The frequently held modern view observes on the other hand that there are good and true things in the other religions of the world, and so many people conclude that each should simply keep his own faith as it is and be quite undisturbed. Yet the first view appears to many in Asia today as representing Western imperialism in a religious guise, and the second view seems to imply a denial of the universality of truth. Therefore let us ask if there is not still another view which may commend itself to us?

This view may be formulated as follows: "Christ is the truth. The other religions have truth, too. He came, not to destroy, but to fulfill." For this view we have the support of the statement of Jesus himself as recorded in Matthew 5:17: "I have come not to abolish . . . but to fulfill." That was spoken with relationship to what from the point of view of Christianity we would now call one of the other religions of the world, namely, Judaism. Jesus was referring to the law and the prophets, the most important parts of the scriptures of the Jewish religion. He declared that he did not come to destroy them but to fulfill them. The word fulfill means to fill full, to complete, to accomplish the intention of. It is our belief that Jesus Christ did that in relation to Judaism. Out of all the laws of the Torah, he picked with unerring insight the two about loving God and loving one's neighbor as oneself. Thus he summed it all up in two central principles. Again, the law contained regulations for a system of sacrifices which had to be made over and over again. But when Christ laid down his life on Calvary, men felt that a perfect sacrifice had been offered which obviated the necessity of the repetition of the old animal sacrifices. So that to which the Jewish religion had been pointing was summed up and perfected in Christ. As Paul put it in Galatians 3:24, the law was our schoolmaster to bring us to Christ, or our custodian until he came. This, essentially, is what is taught in the New Testament of the relationship of Christ to Judaism.

By around A.D. 200 when Christianity had gone out into the Greek world there was a Christian thinker who said substantially this same thing regarding the relationship of Christ and the Hellenistic religion. This was Clement of Alexandria, and here is what he wrote:

> Perchance, too, philosophy was given to the Greeks directly till the Lord should call the Greeks also. For this was a schoolmaster to bring the Hellenic mind to Christ, as was the law to bring the Hebrews. Philosophy, therefore, was a preparation, paving the way for him who is perfected in Christ.

Clement was saying, in effect, that Jesus Christ did not come to destroy the philosophy of the Greeks, but to fulfill it. You could begin at the point of Greek philosophy, and when you came to know about Christ you would find that what you were seeking was realized in him. Actually, in the Christianity of later centuries there was preserved not a little both of Jewish religion and of Greek philosophy, and who will not say that Christianity is the richer for it?

Now once again in our day, Christianity has gone on out into Asia and all the world. Christians are face to face with Buddhism, with Hinduism, and with the philosophies and religions of the rest of the world. May it not be that here, too, Christ will not so much destroy as fulfill? May there not be meanings in these religions which will be made clearer, and may there not be elements which they will contribute, which will give us a fuller understanding of the meaning of Christ?

To take the position that Christ has not come to abolish but to fulfill all that is best in all the religions of the world, is to believe that he is mature. It was Max Müller, I think, who remarked that we ought not say that there is any false religion, any more than we should say that a child is a false man. But the religion of Christ is, as one scholar has called it, "the religion of maturity." It is an ideal which may be held up to the whole world, that we should all come "to mature manhood, to the measure of the stature of the fullness of Christ."[6]

Yet Christ will not win the world unless his followers not only believe in him but also actually manifest something of his spirit and character in the midst of the world. In A. J. Cronin's *The Keys of the Kingdom,* the missionary priest, Father Chisholm, is anxious to win the Chinese people to Christ, but not too anxious. Mr. Chia, a man of wealth, has not been convinced, even by the healing of his son, that Christianity is better than the old religions of China. After many years, however, he comes at last to the priest and says: "My friend, I have often said: There are many religions and each has its gate to heaven. Now it would appear that I have the extraordinary desire to enter by your gate." The priest replies: "I cannot believe that you are serious." And Mr. Chia says: "Once, many years ago, when you cured my son, I was not serious. But then I was unaware of the nature of your life . . . of its patience, quietness, and courage. The goodness of a religion is best judged by the goodness of its adherents. My friend . . . you have conquered me by example."[7]

Only by such examples will Christ win in the world.

CHAPTER TWELVE

The Uniqueness of the Incarnation

In the immediately preceding chapters we have presented the New Testament teaching that God was in Christ, and have suggested that his saying that he came not to destroy the law and the prophets may also be applied to his relation to the other religions of the world. Now, however, we must face the further fact that many of the other religions also claim that manifestations of God have taken place to which they can bear witness. Hinduism is most explicit and emphatic about this. Hinduism declares that God has come to earth in some form in every era, and that there have thus been many incarnations. In the Bhagavad Gita the Lord says, "Whensoever piety languisheth, and impiety doth prevail, I create myself. I am born age after age for the preservation of the righteous, the destruction of evildoers, and the establishment of virtue."

Surprisingly enough, we may agree with this teaching and not be out of line with the thought of some of the greatest Christian writers. "In the beginning was the Word," declares the author of the Fourth Gospel in his stately prologue, and continues, "In him was life and the life was the light of men." Then in the ninth verse, according to the King James Version, he affirms, "That was the true Light, which lighteth every man that cometh into the world." According to that, the Light which is the Word of God can have shone in many places, and been apprehended at least in part by many men. Justin Martyr, who wrote around A.D. 150, says this:

> We have been taught that Christ is the first-born of God, and we have declared above that he is the Word of whom every race of men partake; and those who lived reasonably [that is to say, who lived according to the Word] were Christians, even though they have been thought atheists; as among the Greeks, Socrates and Heraclitus, and those like them; and among the Barbarians, Abraham and Ananias . . . and Azarias, and many others. . . . For whatever either lawgivers or philosophers uttered well they elaborated by finding and contemplating some part of the Word.

Nicholas of Cusa, writing in the Middle Ages, states: "God is sought in various ways and called by various names in the various religions; he has sent various prophets and teachers in various ages to the various peoples." And Thomas Aquinas took up the saying of Ambrose: "Every truth, by whomever it is spoken, is of the Holy Spirit."[1]

While Christianity is thus prepared, according to many of its most respected interpreters, to recognize that the illuminative Word has manifested itself in many places, it also declares in the language of the prologue of the Fourth Gospel that the Word became flesh and dwelt among us in the person of Jesus Christ. In what, then, does the uniqueness of the incarnation in Christ consist?

Historical Rather Than Mythical

Comparing what we have in Christianity first with what we find in the mythological religions, we may say that the incarnation in Jesus Christ is historical rather than mythical. There have been many religions which found their expression in terms of myth. These represent projections of the hopes and longings of men in symbolic form. Here are some examples:

In the Old Testament we often read about the god Baal who was worshiped by the Canaanites. From archeological discovery at Ras Shamra on the Syrian coast, a library of texts which tell about the god Baal has been obtained from an ancient temple. From them we learn that he was the god of the storm. In them it is told how Baal was slain and how his sister Anath mourned for him, and how eventually it came about that he was raised up and made to live again. Then once again the rains poured down on the parched soil of Syria, because Baal, the god of the storm, was again alive.

In Egypt they told the story of Osiris, who was slain by his enemy, Set. His sorrowing wife Isis sought for his body, and when she found it, all dismembered, she gathered the pieces together and Osiris was revived. As we read this story we learn that Isis wept as she went seeking the slain Osiris, wept until the Nile overflowed its banks. So we see that in this myth the great cycle of nature was reflected and the annual inundation which refertilized the Nile valley was described in a symbolic way.

The Greeks told about Demeter and her daughter

Persephone who was abducted by the god of the underworld. After a time Persephone was set free and came back. Demeter mourned while her daughter was away, and the crops languished and failed. When Persephone returned, Demeter rejoiced and the crops grew again. But Persephone had eaten some of the food of the underworld, and so had to go back there for several months every year. So every year the crops and vegetation died, and then after a time lived again.

Such are some of the myths which were told by the ancient Canaanites, Egyptians, and Greeks. One looks upon the hopes and longings of these early peoples with sympathy and understanding, but no one supposes that the personages who figure in these myths really lived. The stories narrated about them clearly reveal that it is events of nature which are reflected in these deities. The death and rebirth of vegetation inspired in men the hope of life after death and led to the telling of the stories of how Baal, Osiris, and others experienced death and life again.

Of all the differences between the mythological religions and Christianity one of the greatest is that Jesus Christ really lived. We know about him in history, so definitely that we can deal with the dates of his life and ascertain that he was born while Herod the Great was still king of the Jews, and at the time when Augustus was ruling the Roman empire; that he began his public work in the fifteenth year of the Emperor Tiberius; that he was crucified when Pontius Pilate was procurator of Judea, probably on the seventh of April in A.D. 30. We discern a historical sequence in what is recorded that he did. He came into conflict with the religious leaders of the Jews. He was accused of being a revolutionist. He was executed as a criminal by the Roman procurator. We see the character of his life. He was born in a stable, worked in a carpenter shop, walked across the land, sometimes slept in a boat, was hungry, tired, thirsty, wrathful, sorrowful. He loved little children, he enjoyed being at a banquet, he was a friend of publicans and sinners, who had no one else for their friend. His life fits exactly into the background of first-century Palestine. We see its villages and walk in its marketplaces when we read about his life. We see its fields and hills, meet its social groups and its religious sects. This one, in whom our hopes are centered, is historical rather than mythical. And of his resurrection, one historian writes: "Surely it is no exaggeration to say that belief in the resurrection of Jesus is the best-attested fact of ancient history."[2]

Universal Rather Than Limited

Next, comparing Christianity with what we may call the national religions of the world, we may say that the incarnation in Jesus Christ is universal rather than limited. There are many religions of limited scope. Either by the intention of their founders or the history of their followers, they have put walls around themselves and been limited to certain areas and groups of people. Moses was a great lawgiver, and we benefit still from principles which he enunciated, yet the Mosaic legislation was, after all, intended for a chosen people, and they themselves have been reluctant to admit outsiders to their number. Zoroaster was the prophet of light against darkness, but the fire that burns in Zoroastrian temples today to symbolize that light is accessible only to the members of a very small community. Hinduism has a great tolerance, and yet its practice is really limited to those who belong to the caste structure of Hindu society. Mahavira, who launched the movement of the Jains, set up such strict ascetic rules that only men can follow them, and according to the teachings of that religion, if you are a woman, you can be saved only by going through this existence and later on being born a man. Lao Tzu and Confucius enunciated elevated philosophies, but they were promulgated for the most part within the limits of China, and do not seem to have been thought of as an evangel for all. Nanak founded the movement of the Sikhs, and said that we should treat everybody as equal, but his followers have been a fiercely patriotic, separate group.

Over against such limitations, the incarnation in Jesus Christ is of universal significance. In the long run there surely cannot be one religion for one part of the world, and another for another, for truth is for all. There cannot be one kind of science in one part of the world and a different kind in another. The law of gravity is the same in the East as in the West. The principles of atomic energy are the same in both places. In the long run it does not look as if there can be democracy in one part of the world, and something diametrically opposed to it in another. In religion, too, therefore, there must ultimately be a universal truth.

Consider then how there were no limits around what Jesus did and taught, even as there have been no limits to where his followers have believed they should go on his behalf, preaching the gospel. Men and women alike were among his disciples and evidently were treated just alike. This is more amazing than we may think, since we live when the influence of that way of doing has been at work in the world for nineteen hundred years. But in that day one rabbi said, "Better that the words of the law should be burned than delivered to women"; and even today in the prayer book of the orthodox Jewish synagogue the prayer still stands, "Blessed art thou, O Lord our God, King of the universe, who hast not made me a woman."

But in the teachings of Jesus there was no limitation. He did wonderful deeds equally for a Jewish widow and for a Roman centurion. There was no wall of division which he did not overpass. Fundamentally the only condition for his blessing was that of faith, and that is a condition which is tied to no nation, no race, and no class. Harry Emerson Fosdick has remarked that there were two major approaches to a cosmopolitan world view in Jesus' day, as in our own. One dealt with the outward facts of political and economic interdependence and came to see the world as one; the other so valued persons, regardless of color, race, or nationality, that all personalities, wherever found, were equally regarded as worth living and dying for. "How far the outward approach may have influenced Jesus none can tell, but that the inward approach, by way of care for individuals, led him to a universal outlook seems plain. Jesus' thought of every soul as infinitely precious in the sight of God was one of his incontestable characteristics. Adolf

Harnack even said: 'Jesus Christ was the first to bring the value of every human soul to light.' "[3]

So in him we find that true universalism which begins with the individual and thus has to do with all persons. The teaching of Jesus is for everybody. There are no lines drawn around it, and it is not confined within narrow boundaries of any kind. He is at home everywhere; his word comes to all men because it comes with the impact of truth to each man.

Absolute Rather Than Partial

Once again we have to face the fact that there are prophetic and missionary religions in the world outside of Christianity, such as Islam and Buddhism. Here we may say that the incarnation in Jesus Christ is absolute rather than partial.

An illustration frequently used by those who study the different religions of the world is that of the mountain peak. The paths, they say, which lead from the base of the mountain toward its summit start from different points but converge as they ascend. Those who climb upon these paths come closer together the farther they go. On the summit they all see at last the same God. But is there anyone yet who has stood upon the summit except Jesus Christ? Is it not because he has stood there that we sense in him and his words what is absolute?

The teaching which he gave has an absolute quality. One cannot think of anything that could be higher. Muhammad, the founder of Islam, lived six hundred years after Christ, and by that test might be thought to supersede Jesus Christ, but actually in his teaching is found a retrogression rather than a progression from what Jesus taught. The Qur'ān, for example, allows each man in Islam four wives. Jesus teaches that "a man shall leave his father and mother and be joined to his wife, and the two shall become one."[4] Some may think that this states an ideal that is too hard, and that cannot always be lived out, yet we cannot see anything higher than this ideal and it does not appear how any more lofty principle could ever be enunciated in this area. To take another example, the injunction to love one's neighbor as oneself is found in the Mosaic religion, but there it is restricted within the limits of the people to whom the Mosaic law was addressed: "You shall not . . . bear any grudge against the sons of your own people, but you shall love your neighbor as yourself."[5] When Jesus restates this command he omits any restriction. His teaching is lifted to the level of the absolute.

There is an absolute obedience in Jesus Christ. The one who became the Buddha went out seeking as in a desperate search, and swung from one extreme to another until he found the great enlightenment. But Jesus at the age of twelve was about his Father's business; facing temptation he said that he must do the Father's will; and praying in Gethsemane he asked that the cup might be taken from him, but if not, that God's will might be done. He was tested, troubled, but always true. As the candle is obedient to the greater fire which lights it and is itself made one with the greater fire, so in Christ there is such an absolute obedience to God that it is the radiance of the Father which shines in the Son.

There is also in Christ an absolute sacrifice. Many

others have laid hold on some portion of the Word, yet none has made the complete sacrifice which Jesus made. Moses died in peace, after a long life, on the threshold of the promised land. Gautama Buddha passed away at the age of eighty, surrounded by his favorite disciples. Confucius died a natural death, over seventy years of age, idolized by many devoted pupils. Muhammad was over sixty years old when he breathed his last, reclining on the breast of his favorite wife, Ayesha. Only Jesus Christ walked out in comparative youth to a lonely hill and a cruel cross and laid down his life in an unforgettable sacrifice.

Because of the quality of his teachings and life and death, Jesus has exercised a compelling influence upon men. Justin Martyr believed that the Word was apprehended in part by Socrates and others, but recognized that Jesus had elicited a greater devotion than any. "For no one," he wrote, "trusted in Socrates so as to die for this doctrine, but in Christ, who was partially known even by Socrates (for he was and is the Word who is in every man . . .), not only philosophers and scholars believed, but also artisans and people entirely uneducated, despising both glory and fear and death; since he is the power of the ineffable Father, and not the mere instrument of human reason." Some years after writing these words, Justin himself rendered the last tribute of loyalty when at Rome, under Rusticus the prefect, he was scourged and beheaded rather than abandon his faith in Jesus Christ.

CHAPTER THIRTEEN

The Acceptance and Rejection of Christ in the World

In spite of all that we have said about the unique incarnation of the Word in Jesus Christ, we have to face the fact that he has been rejected as well as accepted in the world. Paul makes a statement of this fact in I Corinthians 1:22-24: "Jews demand signs and Greeks seek wisdom, but we preach Christ crucified, a stumbling-block to Jews and folly to Gentiles, but to those who are called, both Jews and Greeks, Christ the power of God and the wisdom of God."

The Rejection of Jesus by the Jews

Why did the Jews reject Christ? Jesus worked among the Jewish people, he was one of them. He hardly went outside of Palestine in his entire life. He told his disciples to go through the towns of Israel and to preach to the lost sheep of the house of Israel. We think of him as fulfilling the Old Testament and all that is best in the hopes and expectations of the Jewish religion. But the Jewish people rejected Christ. As John 1:11 puts it, with pathos in the words, "He came to his own home, and his own people received him not." Why did the Jews reject him?

Paul gives us a clue when he says that the Jews required a sign. What kind of sign were they looking for that Christ did not give them? They were looking for the sign of something spectacular. Many spectacular events are narrated in the Old Testament. Moses was validated as the deliverer of the children of Israel from the land of Egypt by the signs which he wrought. Undoubtedly it was expected that Jesus, if he were indeed the Christ, would perform outwardly spectacular deeds. At one time the Pharisees came seeking a sign from him, but Jesus only sighed deeply and said that no sign would be given to that generation. In his temptation he had already faced the suggestion that he base his ministry upon the doing of such things as the turning of stones into bread, and the casting of himself down from the temple, and he had refused such expedients as not in harmony with the will of God. So it must be that the Jews failed to believe in him, at least in part, because he did not do the spectacular deeds widely expected of the Messiah. How about ourselves? What if we go through all our lives without ever seeing something of a spectacularly supernatural character take place? Shall we still believe in Christ, or do we too have to have some outward sign? Many in that day wanted such a proof.

Another sign that the Jewish people wanted to see was the sign of the conquest of their enemies. The second Psalm speaks about the messianic king and says:

> Why do the nations conspire? . . .
> You shall break them with a rod of iron,
> and dash them in pieces like a potter's vessel.

Pick up a pot and throw it down, so that it shatters into a hundred pieces, like the potsherds we now pick up all over Palestine. That is what the messianic king was going to do to the enemies of the Jewish people. If anybody ever had a right to hope that that would happen, it was the Jewish people, with all they had been through. Antiochus Epiphanes had persecuted them, the Romans had come and conquered them. One after another, foreign powers had overwhelmed them. Surely, the Messiah when he came would do the great deed of casting down these enemies and smiting them as they deserved. If Christ had done that, he would doubtless have had a very great following. The others of his time who attempted it, were followed by many. This was true of Judas who headed the Maccabean uprising, of the Zealots who inspired the Jewish war in A.D. 66, and of Bar Cochba who led the rebellion of A.D. 132. The highest point in the popularity of Jesus was probably at the time when the people thought he could be constrained to assume the role of a military leader. John 6:15 reports that "they were about to come and take him by force to make him king," but that he withdrew and went apart into the hills by himself.

We too may be inclined to think that God ought to work that way through Christ. He ought to reach out and smite all the enemies that we have in the world. Martin Luther was greatly attracted to the second Psalm. He said:

> I love this Psalm with all my heart. It strikes and flashes valiantly among kings, princes, counselors, judges, etc. If I were as our Lord God, and had committed the government to my son, as he to his son, and the vile people (who oppose him) were as disobedient as now they be, I would knock the world to pieces.

How about it—can we believe in Christ if we do not see God knock the world to pieces through him? If evildoers still flourish? It was part of the problem for the Jewish people that Jesus did not destroy their enemies.

Another sign that they required in their thinking was the condemnation of sinners. If life was to be lived according to the laws of God there must be penalties for transgression. The heart of these laws is the Ten Commandments. They are found in the twentieth chapter of Exodus. If one reads on only into the following chapter one encounters some of the statements of penalties. For example: "Whoever strikes a man so that he dies shall be put to death. Whoever strikes his father or mother shall be put to death. Whoever steals a man shall be put to death. Whoever curses his father or his mother shall be put to death." Soon after that, one finds the enunciation of the principle of retaliation: "Eye for eye, tooth for tooth, hand for hand, foot for foot, burn for burn, wound for wound, stripe for stripe." The Old Testament contains many cases of the application of severe punishments. One man gathered sticks on the sabbath, thus breaking the law which required rest on that day. He was brought outside the camp and stoned to death. Achan took of prohibited spoil in war, "and all Israel stoned him with stones."[1] Against that background, it is not surprising if there was a widespread expectation that the Messiah, as the representative of the righteousness of God, would be terrible in the condemnation of sinners. But Jesus was merciful to sinners. Therefore the Jewish people missed seeing one of the signs that they expected to see in the Christ.

Another sign that their thinking generally required was the sign of long life. That was the evidence of God's favor. Did not Psalm 91:16 promise, "With long life I will satisfy him, and show him my salvation"? Would you believe in someone who did not live a long life—whose life was cut off early, as if in indication of God's disfavor?

Yet another sign that they expected was that of freedom from suffering. Was it not said on the one hand, "A thousand may fall at your side, ten thousand at your right hand, but it will not come near you"; and on the other, "A hanged man is accursed by God"?[2] How could they believe in one who was put to death by being nailed upon a cross? Was this not a plain evidence of God's displeasure and condemnation?

Such, then, must have been some of the kinds of signs which Jewish thinking required of the Messiah. Failing to find them in Jesus, it was unable to accept him.

The Rejection of Christ by the Greeks

Why did the Greeks reject Christ? In the case recorded in John 12:20-21, where some Greeks come and say that they wish to see Jesus, we are led to suppose that he, although rejected by the Jews, may be accepted by the Greeks. Out in the Greek world they did not have all of the laws, prohibitions, and restrictions which burdened the Jews. It was a wider world, one of philosophy and freedom of thought. When Christ was made known there, would he not be accepted? But Paul tells us that Christ was rejected by the Greeks, as by the Jews, and again he gives us a clue as to why it was when he says that the Greeks seek wisdom.

What kind of wisdom were the Greeks seeking? What kind of wisdom do we seek when we follow the general line of Greek thought as we commonly do in both philosophy and science? For one thing they sought after universal law, and so do we. This means looking for an abstract truth, or a general description of how things act. But in the case of Jesus Christ we are asked to believe in a specific happening, an unrepeated event, and a unique individual. This is difficult for a Greek-trained mind to do. Lessing, the philosopher, once said: "Accidental historical truths can never be the evidence for eternal and necessary rational truths." Such a type of thought is eager to comprehend general propositions, but it stumbles over an individual event which cannot readily be subsumed under a more inclusive law. The idea is what matters, not the particular man in whom it is embodied. Yet Christianity preaches Christ and him crucified. Such thought seeks abstract truth, yet Jesus is all the time concrete and specific. His teaching is not couched in vague generalities. He answers individual questions and speaks to particular persons.

Again, in their search for wisdom the Greeks thought much about a cyclical universe. The most prevalent theory of history among the Greeks was that the same things happen over and over again. Alternate periods of progress and decline succeed each other ceaselessly. What has happened in the past will happen again in the future. What now is, was before, and will be again. To the mind trained to think in this way, the teaching of Jesus must have come as surprisingly different. Jesus spoke of something new and epoch making which was drawing near, indeed was already at hand, as he preached. This was the kingdom of God, and he also spoke of it as a future definitive consummation. Thus the disciples were led to consider the present moment as of crucial importance and to look forward with hope and affirmative expectation to what lay ahead. A linear quality characterized the Christian message, and this was hard for the Greek mind to comprehend, trained as it was to think in terms of circular movements in history. The conception of a dynamic, active God, concerned about the world and breaking into history was nearly impossible for a Greek to grasp, whose god was Law, Idea, an unmoved Mover.

Furthermore, Greek wisdom was all the time seeking for unmarred beauty and undisturbed harmony. A Greek statue is usually an embodiment of perfection. Everything is in perfect balance and symmetry. That was the Greek ideal. But what could the Greek mind do with Jesus to whom Christians, thinking of the sufferings he endured, felt it appropriate to apply the words of Isaiah 52:14: "his visage was so marred more than any man"?[3]

The Greeks in their thinking were also like many in the modern world in that they believed in moderation. They often said, "Nothing too much." This seems like a rational approach to living—do some of everything and do nothing to excess. Yet in the teaching of Jesus there was a call to do some things in excess of every reasonable requirement. It is excessive to go two miles when you are compelled to go but one, but Jesus told his disciples to do it. It seems excessive to do many of the things which Jesus talks about, and if one's fundamental idea is never to do too much of anything, it is difficult to attain to the radical commitment to which the teaching of Jesus is a summons.

Once more, the Greeks in their wisdom aimed at self-knowledge. Their motto was, "Know thyself." "Man," they said, "is the measure of all things." This puts man at the center of the universe. But in the teaching of Jesus it is not man but God who occupies that central position. Man's life has meaning only as he has faith in God and lives according to the will of God. Accordingly Greek wisdom stumbled over the acceptance of Christ.

The Acceptance of Christ

In the foregoing we have noted a number of reasons that Christ was rejected by Jews and Greeks, and in doing so have at the same time actually given reasons that he is still rejected, since we today still follow many of the lines of Jewish and Greek thought.

But it was the conviction of Paul that Christ, although he seemed a stumbling block to the Jews and folly to the Greeks, was in reality the power and the wisdom of God. Against the background of the preceding analysis, we may indicate briefly some of the ways in which this is true.

The Jews sought an outward sign, but the simple, stupendous fact of the life of Jesus is the greatest sign of all. What if he had done some of the things which were expected, such as throwing himself off the pinnacle of the temple? It is doubtful if it would mean much to the world today. But the kind of life he lived, of spiritual stature and greatness, in which God shines through, means a great deal. "He in his own person is the 'sign of the time,' " declares Rudolf Bultmann.[4] What was immensely significant was not outward signs that he did, but the sign that he was.

He did not conquer their enemies as the Jews wanted him to do. He forgave them, and thereby he conquered them most effectively of all. It is related of Abraham Lincoln that once when he said some kind words about the Confederates, a woman asked him how he could speak kindly of his enemies when he ought rather to try to destroy them. Lincoln replied, "What, Madam! Do I not destroy them when I make them my friends?"

Jesus did not condemn sinners, he forgave them. It was expected that he would condemn, and on one occasion one person was brought before him with the expectation that he would acquiesce in her stoning. Instead he sent her away without condemnation. Jesus Christ comes to us, not to condemn but to forgive us. For any sins we are doubtless condemned already in the court of our own conscience, and punished in unavoidable consequences. But he comes to forgive, to lift up, and to give a new chance.

It was not the quantity of his life, it was the quality. What if he had lived for eighty years or more? Methuselah is said to have lived 969 years, but nothing is told of any accomplishment in all that time. Jesus lived little more than thirty years, but it was the quality of those years, not the quantity of them, which mattered.

He was not free from suffering, but as a matter of fact he took suffering upon himself. He not only endured it, he used it. It seemed a reproach, yet his cross has become the symbol of our faith.

The Greeks sought a general principle, but the life of Christ was a unique event. In all the general principles there are, we have to get hold of something that is really there. And there is really in the life of Christ something uniquely wonderful in the history of this world. Rebecca E. Pitts wrote:

> No one can read the New Testament narratives in an unprejudiced mood . . . without perceiving a core of stubborn, intractable fact. It is not myth, but another kind of mystery, that environs the most moving moments and events. Therefore we dare not doubt the impact of a tremendous Life, so overwhelming in its meaning and influence that legends are merely the symbolic jewels . . . with which later minds adorn its memory.[5]

There was in Christ inspiration and influence upon men to set them free from the pernicious influence of cyclical pessimism and to cause them to move forward. In Christ there was not indeed the unmarred beauty of a Greek statue in its perfection, but the greater beauty of a wounded hand. There was not the cautious ethics of "nothing too much," but the exuberant and almost incredible ethics of the Sermon on the Mount. There was not the proud assurance that man could stand all by himself, but there was a full dependence upon God, in whom Jesus himself lived, and whose radiance shone through him.

For all these reasons which are really answers to the difficulties that the Jew and the Greek found in Christ, both Jews and Greeks can believe in him. Both Jews and Greeks have done so. It is unfair to say that the Jews rejected Christ. Many of them did, but many of them accepted him. Who were the first disciples? Who were the twelve? Who were the members of the Jerusalem church? Who was Paul? All were Jews and all were believers in Christ.

It is unfair to say that the Greeks rejected him, en masse. Some did. But many others believed. The Syrophoenician woman whom Jesus blessed, Titus who was a companion of Paul, Justin who became a martyr for his faith, and many more, were Greeks. To all those who are called, as Paul declares, both Jews and Greeks, and to all of us in whose heritage elements are blended from both the Old Testament and Greek philosophy, and who find in him the fulfillment of the intimations and aspirations of both sources, Christ is the power of God and the wisdom of God.

CHAPTER FOURTEEN

The Miracles of Christ

In the study of the life of Jesus, should we pay any attention to the miracles which he is reported to have done? Are the miracles important?

The Importance of the Miracles

It is certainly true that the miracles are not the most important thing in the life of Christ. According to the records, he himself minimized their place in his own work. In his temptation he refused to perform miracles when it was suggested to him that he do so. When Pharisees sought a sign from him, he said that no sign would be given to that generation. When enormous crowds gathered after he performed healings at Capernaum, he rose very early the next morning and went away. He went out to a desert place alone, apart from the crowds eager to see miracles, and prayed. When he did heal people, he often instructed them not to tell anyone else what had happened. He always made it plain that faith must rest upon something deeper than signs and wonders.

It is also true that different views are held concerning the miracles by honest students and sincere and conscientious Christians. Some persons look at miracles from the point of view of skepticism. Their definition of miracles is that they are things which never happened. One person remarks that if a modern man were to see Jesus walking on the water, instead of falling down and worshiping him, he would say, "Pardon me, sir, would you mind doing that again, so I can see how you did it?" Howard Thurman tells about a classmate of his who gave a senior sermon on the significance of Jesus in his life. He said, "I do not believe he walked on water; I do not believe he turned water into wine; I do not believe any of the miracles recorded in the Gospels. For me this is unnecessary. But, when I look at his life and contrast it with my own, I am perfectly willing to call him God. A wide, wide gulf separates me from him."[1]

Others look at the accounts of the miracles of Christ as legends. They think they can understand how these stories grew up. Legends are narratives which are formulated in order to enhance the importance of a person or event in the past. Thus the existence of these stories concerning miracles which Christ performed is really a testimony to the significance of his life.

There are those, too, who look at the miracles from the point of view of rationalism. They believe that by careful scrutiny of the records it is possible to discern the natural happenings which gave rise to these miraculous narratives. Thus, for example, where it is recorded that Jesus performed the miracle of feeding five thousand people, what really happened, they explain, was that a boy in the crowd had brought a lunch, as some other people had not, when they rushed off to that desert place. Seeing one beside him without anything to eat, the lad shared his lunch. Others caught this spirit and did likewise. Jesus perhaps blessed what was done as they shared in that way, and it came to be told that he had multiplied the loaves and fishes into enough for all. Similarly, in the case of the transfiguration, it is held that Jesus interviewed two men on a mountain top. The clouds blew over, the sun shone through, and Jesus looked as if he were irradiated. In the case of the raising of a man from the dead, the person was in fact only in a coma anyway. These are rationalistic explanations, and to such a rationalist as H. E. G. Paulus, for example, all the miracles consist merely in the fact that eyewitnesses have reported events the secondary causes of which they did not know. Our only problem, accordingly, is to discover the secondary causes.

Once again, the miracle narratives are viewed by some as allegories. Those who hold this view explain that the miracle stories got started in the spiritual experience of the early Christians, that they are told to express that spiritual experience, and should be read for the spiritual truth which they convey. For example, the story of the calming of the storm on the Sea of Galilee expresses the fact that Christ stills the storm within our hearts, and brings peace. It also suggests that although the church is only a little ship tossed upon the stormy waves of the world, we need not be afraid, for Christ is on board, and he is not asleep. He will quiet the storm and bring the vessel safely to port. As John Knox puts it: "The miracle stories were believed, remembered, and loved because the wonderful power of Christ was a present reality in the life of the community; they were used in preaching because they embodied and conveyed this reality."[2]

For ourselves, however, it is desired to take a realistic view of the miracles of Christ and to ask seriously whether he did such things as are reported in the Gospels. Such an attempt to get the actual facts is a necessary part of our total endeavor to understand Christ. In so doing it must be recognized that there was a tendency to tell more and more stories about marvelous things which Christ did. If we turn to the apocryphal gospels, we can observe this growth of miracle stories plainly. In the apocryphal gospel of Thomas, for example, it is told that when Jesus was a little child five years old, he made sparrows out of the soft clay by the side of the brook. Joseph rebuked him because he did this on the sabbath. He clapped his hands, and the clay sparrows flew away. Again, when he was eight years old, he was helping Joseph in the carpenter shop. They made a bed. One beam was too short. He took hold of it and stretched it until it was long enough to match the other one. One has no hesitation in thinking that these are just stories. They were doubtless told with an earnest desire to do honor to Jesus, but we would doubt today if such narratives did very much honor to him. Since the tendency to heighten the miraculous is unmistakably evident in the apocryphal literature, it may well have been at work already in the time when the canonical Gospels were composed.

But if, now, it be supposed that it is possible to work back from these late miracle-filled narratives to early records which are devoid of the miraculous and in which Jesus appears as a perfectly ordinary person possessed of no special powers, that is emphatically not the case. The oldest of the Gospels in the New Testament is almost certainly that according to Mark, since it was evidently used as an outline and a source of narrative material by the authors of Matthew and Luke. But Mark, the oldest Gospel, is scarcely less than a rapid-fire account of the marvelous things Jesus did. Often linked together by the word "immediately,"[3] one reads section after section of narrative concerning wonderful deeds. Immediately on the sabbath, Jesus was in the synagogue, and there was a man there with an unclean spirit, and he healed him. Immediately he went to Simon's house where Simon's mother-in-law lay sick with a fever, and he lifted her up and the fever left. As soon as the sun went down and the enforced rest of the sabbath was over, they brought to him all who were sick or possessed with demons and he healed many.

Older even than Mark, probably, is a collection of the sayings of Jesus which is usually held to lie back of the quotations of his teachings which are found in almost identical form in the Gospels according to Matthew and according to Luke. Since in many of the narrative sections which Matthew and Luke have in common it can be demonstrated that they depended upon Mark, the existence of common sections of discourse material in the two Gospels suggests the employment here too of a source accessible to both authors. Since this hypothetical source must have been primarily a collection of sayings, and probably originated quite early, we might expect to find in it evidence for nothing except the work of Jesus as a great teacher. But actually, as the sayings source is usually reconstructed, it contained the account of the healing of the centurion's servant; the reply to John the Baptist about the blind given sight, the lame made to walk, the lepers cleansed, the deaf made to hear, and the dead raised up; the answer to the accusation that Jesus was driving out demons by Beelzebul, and the statement that if it was by the finger of God he was casting out demons, then the kingdom of God was come upon men; and the reference to the unclean spirit gone out of a man and afterward come back with seven others worse than itself.[4] All these materials have to do with miraculous things which Jesus did, and all are in one of our oldest available sources concerning Jesus. So it does not appear to be possible to get far enough back to find Jesus portrayed with no reference to the miraculous. At the farthest point back to which we can get, Jesus is pictured as doing things which we ordinarily call miracles.[5]

New Clues for Understanding

Since the report of miracles is inextricably connected with the record of the life of Jesus, we have next to ask if there are any new clues which may help us in the attempt to understand what really happened. With this inquiry in view, let us divide the miracles into several groups as to kind. For one group, there are what we may call the miracles of knowing. These involve accounts where Jesus is said to have known what was in the mind of other persons, without their speaking, or to have known what happened at some place where he was not present. According to Luke 6:8, when he healed the man with the withered hand in the synagogue, the scribes and Pharisees watched him with sinister intent, "but he knew their thoughts." In John 4:39 the Samaritan woman reported, "He told me all that I ever did." According to John 11:14, Jesus knew of the death of his friend Lazarus in the distant village of Bethany although the only word that had come was the report of his illness received two days before.

Now, we may say that these are legends intended to make us appreciate how great a person Jesus was. We may rationalize the accounts and say that Jesus saw the look on the men's faces in the synagogue, and thus perceived what they were thinking about. He was told how sick Lazarus was, and from the symptoms made a prognosis of death in two days which he announced to the disciples only after that length of time and which turned out to be correct. Or we may interpret the accounts allegorically and emphasize the intimate knowledge which Christ has of us. But did something really happen? Did Jesus have a special knowledge of the thoughts of people, of what they were like, of what they had done, and of what happened even at a distance? The new clue which makes this seem more possible is the modern study of the special, occasionally found faculty of the human mind that does actually, by experimental tests, as it seems from evidence thus far reported, sometimes reach out across space and even time, without the use of the usual sensory channels, and hence is known as extrasensory perception.

Next there are the miracles of healing. Of these there are so many that we cannot even undertake to list them. They are in all the Gospels. As we consider them is there any new clue available for their understanding? The clue given by modern psychosomatic medicine is relevant to the study of these miracles. We now have a fresh appreciation of the fact that the mind and spirit on the one hand, and the body on the other are intimately interrelated and that one's sins, wrath, remorse, anger, or cherished bitterness, can have repercussions of a physical sort. They can ruin health and cause diseases which can never be healed simply by the surgeon's knife or any kind of pills, but only by getting back to where one lives, to where one's thoughts are, and to where the root of the trouble is. It may be, therefore, that Jesus was dealing in the realm of these interrelationships, and applying mental and spiritual powers to accomplish physical healing. Leslie D. Weatherhead has written:

> In my opinion, the healing miracles represent the normal activities of a Person living on that high plane of experience and of communion with God. So far from being a breach of law . . . they illustrate the scope and wealth of law, and point to the fact that even on this higher plane . . . there is cosmos and law, and never chaos and confusion.[6]

It is true that many of the stories of healing are told in terms of the casting out of demons. This simply corresponds with the common conception of that day, a conception which we have of course left behind. Yet when it is recalled that there are 376,000 beds in general hospitals in the United States of America but 430,000 for nervous and mental diseases, we can scarcely boast of superior mental health just because we no longer hold to the theory of demon possession. As S. Vernon McCasland remarks in his book, *By the Finger of God,* "in psychic terms the ancient world is separated from ours only by the exceedingly thin veil of a changed vocabulary." In the same book he proceeds to a thorough investigation of the cases of driving out of demons recorded in the Gospels and claims that the only way in which these can be really understood by the modern student is by interpreting them in terms of psychiatric views of various kinds of insanity. With regard, for example, to the words of the demon to Jesus in Mark 5:7, "I adjure you by God, do not torment me," he writes as follows:

> If we keep in mind that a psychosis is experienced as a state of release and fulfillment by the inhibited and deranged ego, the statement of the demon to Jesus makes good sense just as it stands. Naturally Jesus, who proposes to drive out the demon, that is, to heal the pathological condition, is regarded as an enemy. . . . The sick mind which has thrown off all inhibitions and found freedom in the psychosis now clings desperately to its paradise. In this perspective Mark's report of what the demon said to Jesus sounds realistic and authentic."[7]

Of course, in understanding these miracles we must not forget the central element of faith—the faith of Jesus and the faith of the healed believer. Such faith breeds a new power. In this respect these are revelatory miracles, for they hint at the attitude of mind which will characterize the forthcoming kingdom of God, being here bodied forth in Jesus. They are, at most, an integral part of God's saving and recreating act. At least, they are a profound parable of his activity.[8]

But what about the nature miracles? Of these an

example particularly difficult for the modern mind to deal with is provided by the account of the cursing of the fig tree found in the eleventh chapter of Mark. To a fig tree which gave the appearance of fruitfulness but in actuality had no fruit, Jesus said, "May no one ever eat fruit from you again." The next morning when they passed that way it was seen that the fig tree had withered. The fact that in the parallel version of the story in the twenty-first chapter of Matthew it is said that the fig tree withered away at once as soon as Jesus spoke, may be accounted for by a desire to heighten the miraculous. But what about the event itself? It is in such a case as this that we may most of all feel driven to legend or allegory as an explanation. Yet with the new understanding we have of the interrelationship of mind and body one wonders if there are interrelationships between mind or spirit and the physical universe itself of which we as yet scarcely dream but with which Jesus dealt and which can account for even such an event as this? As a matter of fact there are even reports in our time of experiments in the application of positive and negative prayer to growing plants with results which are in line with the implications of the gospel narrative discussed in the present paragraph.[9]

On the whole, then, in the light of recent investigations in relevant fields we find ourselves less inclined to turn to legendary, rationalistic, or allegorical explanations of the miracles of Christ, and more inclined to feel that we are dealing here with realistic accounts of things which he did in his relations with other people, in his healing of those who were sick, and perchance even in his relationship to the world of nature itself.

A More Wonderful World

In the course of such a study as we have been engaged in in this chapter one is led to the conclusion that the world is more wonderful than we know. It has aspects and dimensions and possibilities that are greater than we commonly realize. We can share the desire of the rationalist to have a natural explanation for all that happens, but we must realize that that which is natural is simply what really is and what actually happens, and we must always take account of facts wherever we encounter them, and expand our own understanding to the measure of the facts as they really are.

Also, we are led to the conclusion that Christ was and is a more wonderful person than we commonly realize. He lived on a high plane, he refused to use special powers for himself, but from time to time, and usually out of love for people in need and in trouble, he did things which in our present state of understanding we can describe only as miracles.

Furthermore, we are led to believe that life itself has more wonderful possibilities than we know or commonly realize, and that it is right and proper in each and every situation, no matter how desperate, to make our prayer to God, and to ask in the name of Jesus Christ for help, with faith, believing that something wonderful and sufficient for us can and will take place. Here are two incidents in contemporary Christian experience, one of which was communicated in a letter from an American pastor, the other of which was given prominence in a national magazine. The American pastor was preaching in early 1954 in South India, and was asked to participate in a service of prayer for the sick. One young woman refused to come into the service but kept somewhat apart, surrounded by a number of people who said she was possessed by a demon. The pastor was asked to go to her, which he did. There was a strange, wild look in her eyes, and when he endeavored to kneel beside her she grew quite frantic and then rolled over on her mat unconscious. He began to pray, and asked in the name of Christ for healing and health for this poor woman. At the end of the prayer she opened her eyes, and they were normal and full of light. A beautiful smile came over her face, and she stretched out her hands for him to lift her to her feet. "I do not know if she was demon-possessed," wrote the American pastor. "All I know is that she was marvelously delivered by the name of Jesus."[10]

In a New Jersey commuter train wreck in 1951, about thirty members of a single church were injured, three were killed, and one other suffered such severe brain injury that he lay in the hospital for days in profound unconsciousness and with slight hope held out for his life. Both this man and his wife sang in the church choir, and the wife's name had already been printed in the program as the soloist for the next Sunday morning. At that point in the course of the Sunday service the pastor was reminded of the sick man and, acting upon impulse, asked the whole congregation to join with him in prayer that Christ would enter that hospital room and lay his hand upon the brow of that man and heal him. Thinking it had been a long prayer, when he finished he noticed the time, 11:20 A.M. Afterward as he was sitting alone in his study, the telephone rang. The wife was calling to say that her husband had opened his eyes, a proposed critical operation would not have to take place, and he was beginning to get well. It had been 11:20 that morning when he opened his eyes.

Wonderful things do happen because God is love and power, and because Christ is close to God. If we come close to him we have blessing and help of some kind coming into our lives. It is not always the way we ask or would plan. In the same train wreck from which one man was marvelously restored, three other church members were killed, and they were doubtless as much loved and needed by their families as the one who got well. But in some way or other there is help for everybody in time of need, through the great power which is in Jesus Christ.[11]

CHAPTER FIFTEEN

Why Did Jesus Die?

After a relatively brief ministry, the life of Jesus was ended by crucifixion. Why did Jesus die?

As Men Saw It

From the point of view of man, a number of answers may be given to this question. The Jewish people of that time would doubtless have said that Jesus had to die because he was a false leader. A statement still preserved in the Talmud concerning Jesus says of him: "On the eve of Passover they hanged Jesus . . . because he practiced sorcery and led Israel astray." Each point in this statement is of much interest. The fact that he was put to death on the eve of Passover agrees with what we are told in the Fourth Gospel and helps us to ascertain the very date of the crucifixion. The allegation that he practiced sorcery reflects the miracles which Jesus did, as they were seen by men who did not believe that they were works done in the love and power of God. That Jesus led Israel astray no doubt reflects the teachings which he gave when he made it plain that man was more important than the sabbath; that what a man ate or did not eat did not matter so much as what came out of his heart; that fasts, ablutions, and other ceremonies were relatively insignificant; that some of the authorities of the Jewish religion were hypocrites; and that such people as publicans and sinners were loved by God and welcome in his kingdom. These were dangerous teachings, and destructive to the system of religion which then prevailed. So Jesus looked like a false leader—so much so that the heads of that religion became his enemies and accomplished his death.

Jesus died, as men saw it, not only because he was a false leader, but also because he was a fanatical leader. The oldest Roman record about Jesus is preserved in the writings of Tacitus. This historian states: "Christ was put to death in the reign of Tiberius by the procurator Pontius Pilate." We know who the procurators were. They were special representatives of the emperor who were sent to places in the Roman empire where conditions were particularly tumultuous. It was because Judea was a turbulent region that a series of procurators exercised authority there from A.D. 6, on. The procurator mentioned by Tacitus, Pontius Pilate, was the fifth in this line of governors. It was the fundamental endeavor of the procurators of Rome to keep order, and therefore in case of anything which looked like unrest or uprising it was their policy to put it down immediately, before it got out of hand. The tendency of things to get out of hand in Palestine was whipped up by the Zealots. These people wanted a rebellion against the Roman authority. From Josephus, the Jewish historian, we know about a number of the Zealots, including Hezekiah, who opposed Herod Antipas; his son Judas the Gaulonite, who rebelled when Quirinius' census was taken; John of Gischala, who started the war in A.D. 66; and Bar Cochba, who said he was the Messiah, and started the last rebellion in A.D. 132. So as the Romans saw it, any threat of uprising was to be put down, and if a fanatical leader appeared on the horizon, he should be done away with. This was the policy of Pilate. When there was unrest, he suppressed it with violence. He mingled the blood of certain Galileans with that of their animal sacrifices. He slaughtered and imprisoned a multitude of Samaritans when they came to Mount Gerizim to search for certain sacred vessels they thought were buried there. So when Jesus was accused before Pilate with the words, "We found this man perverting our nation, and forbidding us to give tribute to Caesar, and saying that he himself is Christ a king,"[1] he was made to appear to the Roman authorities like a fanatical leader and dangerous person, and that was why he had to die.

As for the people, many of them saw Jesus as a foolish leader. One day some of his friends, as they witnessed the work he was doing, said, "He is beside himself."[2] His mother and his brothers came and sent in to where he was, surrounded by many people, and besought that he come to them. They evidently thought he was foolish in what he was doing. And at the end, the Jerusalem crowds which first hailed him and then cried against him, must have thought that it was foolish of him to behave as he did. So, as it appeared to men, Jesus was obliged to die because he was a false, fanatical, and foolish leader.

What Jesus Thought

Now let us take another viewpoint, and try to see why Jesus died, as he himself looked at it. It may not be possible wholly to penetrate into the thought of Jesus about this, but surely we can get some clues. For one thing, he went to Calvary because it was the will of the Father. Of this we can be sure. Jesus always did the will of his heavenly Father. At the age of twelve he said he must be about his Father's business. In his temptation, he said that he must do the Father's will, and at the last, when he went to dark Gethsemane, he prayed that the cup might pass, but if that were not the Father's will, then he would drink it indeed. Jesus surely knew what God's will was, better than anybody else ever did, and so if he felt and knew within himself that it was the will of God that he should die, it must indeed have been so, that in the historical situation and in the human situation it was necessary for Jesus to die, in order that God's purpose be worked out.

We also think that Jesus saw his death as the work of the "servant." It is more difficult to be sure about this, but we do know that Jesus studied the Scriptures and knew them well; that he found in them guidance for his own life and work; and thus it seems likely that as he studied the Scriptures of his people he found in them the passages which spoke about the "suffering servant." When he was baptized, the Gospels record that he heard a voice in which God spoke to him, saying he was his beloved Son with whom he was well pleased.[3] These words actually echo two statements which are in the Old Testament. "You are my son," is found in Psalm 2:7, and is what God says to the Messianic king. "With thee I am well pleased" is probably from Isaiah 42:1, where God speaks of his servant as one "in whom my soul delights." The last passage, however, is only one of a series of "servant songs," which come to a climax in the fifty-third chapter of the same book with a description of the servant as a man of sorrows, who has borne our griefs, who was wounded for our transgressions, and who was bruised for our iniquities. So it may well have been that in these passages Jesus came to see his death as the work of the servant.

Also, he saw it as the way of the new covenant. When the Scriptures of the Jewish people told about the old covenant which God made with their forefathers, it was related that Moses took the blood of the sacrificial animals, threw it upon the people, and said, "Behold the blood of the covenant which the Lord has made with you."[4] Then Jesus, at the Last Supper with his disciples said, as he passed them the cup, "This is my blood of the covenant, which is poured out for many."[5] So we conclude that Jesus looked at his death as the will of God, as the work of the servant of God, and as the way of establishing a new covenant, a new relationship between God and man.

The Purpose of God

If Jesus believed that it was the will of God that he should die, then we must ask what was the purpose of God in his death? At once we must say that the love of God stood behind the whole redemptive work, a love which could satisfy itself only in redemptive effort. Human minds can hardly hope to know fully the purpose of God, yet the Apostle Paul has ventured to say some things on the subject, and in general we feel that he had a deep understanding of the significance of Jesus and of the relationship between God and man. The first thing Paul says which bears on this matter is that we have all sinned and fallen short. In the opening chapters of Romans he points to the Gentiles and declares that they do many evil things; then he tells about the Jews and observes that whereas they ought to be better than the Gentiles since they have the written law for guidance, they are really worse, since in spite of the advantage of possessing the law they still do wrong. Paul can only conclude, "All have sinned and fall short of the glory of God."[6] In the modern world, with our wars and gross inequalities, we can hardly deny that mankind has gone wrong and has done wrong, and at least many of us individually would have to link ourselves with mankind and confess that we too have done things which are wrong in the sight of God. So Paul says, as a purely factual statement, men are sinners. Every man is born into a humanity that has gone astray, and most of us have made our own concrete transgressions and thereby become jointly responsible. Men have sinned.

The result of this, says Paul in the next place, is the wrath of God. "The wrath of God is revealed from heaven against all ungodliness and wickedness of men who by their wickedness suppress the truth."[7]

This affirmation is just as factual as the foregoing one about sin. Paul does not mean that God gets angry like a bad-tempered person, but he does mean that there is destruction and disaster and ruin because of sin. This he calls the wrath of God. And whether we look at the results of individual faithlessness or of national greed and perfidy in the world today we can hardly deny that Paul is right.

Then what has God done about it? Now Paul comes to the answer we have been seeking. He says: "For our sake he made him to be sin who knew no sin, so that in him we might become the righteousness of God."[8] However, this is not to be taken in a mechanical sense, as an exchange of righteousness for sin. As A. C. Knudsen, in *Basic Issues in Christian Thought,* has reminded us, guilt and merit are inseparable from personality. They cannot be detached from one person and transferred to another. The innocent person cannot become guilty, nor the guilty person become not guilty. However, the guilty may be treated as innocent, and the innocent as guilty; but that is another matter. We are the ones who are sinners and upon whom the load of disaster and ruin rests because of that fact, and it is for our sake that God has done what he has done. Jesus is the one who was not guilty of the sins which weigh down upon mankind. But God, without being separated from the Son, allowed him to be treated as if he were a sinner legally, in order to bring man, dulled and insensitive, face to face with the fact that goodness is willing to die in order to save man from his alienation, from himself. He was put to death as a criminal would be put to death. He was not guilty of our sins but entered into them as completely as if he were: that we in him might become righteous. "Jesus died because man refused to die—to die to self; and to enable man to die. Thus the aim of the cross is reconciliation and forgiveness."[9] There is here certainly no mechanical notion of substitution, appeasement, debt paying, ransom, or erasing of the facts.

Is it not so, that he who would rescue another must often enter into his situation? Someone is drowning in the sea, and another must plunge into the dangerous surf in order to rescue that drowning person. Miners are entombed in the earth because of a cave-in in the mine. Others must go down into those dark and dangerous depths in order to endeavor to get them out. Men are suffering from yellow fever; other men must put themselves into a situation where yellow fever is a danger in order to accomplish the conquest of the dread disease and deliver the sufferers. So Jesus Christ goes into the terrible situation of man's sinfulness, and is treated like a sinner, crucified, and put to death like a criminal, in order to rescue us and bring us salvation. The one loses his life in order that the many may have life. Such, as Paul explains it, was the way God used the death of Jesus for the salvation of man.

It is related that when the body of Abraham Lincoln was lying in state in Cleveland, an elderly Negro woman stood there for a long time with a little child in her arms. Then she said to the child, "Take a long, long look, honey; that man died for you." So the world, looking at the cross of Christ, has come to say, "That Man died for us."

CHAPTER SIXTEEN

The Resurrection and a New Theory of Immortality

The Gospels which tell about the life of Jesus do not end with the account of the crucifixion. They go on to tell of his resurrection, and the rest of the New Testament too is full of references to that fact. As with other subjects which we have discussed, we shall try to understand as much as possible about the resurrection both by studying what is told in the Bible and also by relating what is found there to what man has otherwise learned by exploration of and thought about his universe. In this case we shall begin with general considerations and then turn to specific Bible teachings.

A Theory of Immortality

Already in this book references have been made to the conception of a long process of development which is manifest in the universe, and it has been held that this conception is useful for the understanding of the work of God in creation and of the place of Jesus Christ in history. Now we shall make one further suggestion, and that is that this theory of a long process of development in the universe leads properly to and is incomplete without the further idea of immortality.

For the conception that there is a great process of development going on in the universe we are fundamentally indebted to the work of Darwin and his successors. These men looked at the record of the rocks, the record of fossils, the structure of plants, the anatomy of animals, and saw the marks of interrelationship and progressive change. Darwin's explanation was that this takes place as a process of natural selection through adaptation to environment. The chameleon changes its color to match the background against which it is placed, and thereby survives. Things that live have survived because they have become adapted to their environment. More recently it has been felt that this simple and rather mechanical explanation which used to prevail is insufficient. If adaptation to environment were all that ever took place, then the end result would surely be equilibrium, equipoise, and stagnation. When we ourselves become too comfortably adjusted to things round about us we sometimes begin to stagnate, and it takes a push which thrusts us out of our pleasant situation and destroys our complacency, to get us going ahead again. An idea has been growing among people who think about this, that there is in the process of development in the universe, a push, something which accounts for the fact that again and again at the very point where otherwise stagnation would be expected, some new, unpredictable, and surprising advance takes place. To the process of development seen in this light, Lloyd Morgan gave the name of emergent evolution. Morgan's theory has been stated in essence by Joseph Burgess as follows:

As the evolutionary process has gone on during the ages various stages have been reached when that which actually did not have prior existence "emerged" as something wholly new in the world. When conditions in nature were "favorable," these new forms or variations made their appearance. In this way the organic world emerged from the inorganic, sensation from the insensible, consciousness from the unconscious. In nature there are many levels, each succeeding one being built upon preceding ones but possessing at the same time certain distinguishing emergent characteristics peculiarly its own. Nature is, according to this theory, a graded series, beginning with the most simple orders of existence and extending oppositely to the most complex ones. Low down in the scale are the physical and chemical orders while high in it are the biological and psychological.*[1]

Henri Bergson also was discontented with a mechanistic, mechanical explanation of the development that is going on in the world. He considered that there must be a vital force, a life force, pushing up and pushing on. He called this the *élan vital,* and wrote as follows about "creative evolution":

As the smallest grain of dust is bound up with our entire solar system, drawn along with it in that undivided movement of descent which is materiality itself, so all organized beings, from the humblest to the highest, from the first origins of life to the time in which we are, and in all places as in all times, do but evidence a single impulsion, the inverse of the movement of matter, and in itself indivisible. All the living hold together, and all yield to the same tremendous push. The animal takes

* By permission from *Introduction to the History of Philosophy* by J. B. Burgess. Copyright, 1939. The McGraw-Hill Book Company, Inc.

its stand on the plant, man bestrides animality, and the whole of humanity, in space and in time, is one immense army galloping beside and before and behind each of us in an overwhelming charge able to beat down every resistance and clear the most formidable obstacles, perhaps even death.[2]

Yet another thinker, Lecomte du Noüy, writing of human destiny, used the term "telefinality" and said:

> Following our hypothesis, telefinality orients the march of evolution as a whole and has acted, ever since the appearance of life on earth, as a distant directing force tending to develop a being endowed with a conscience, a spiritually and morally perfect being. To attain its goal, this force acts on the laws of the inorganized world in such a way that the normal play of the second law of thermodynamics is always deflected in the same direction, a direction forbidden to inert matter and leading to ever greater dissymmetries, ever more "improbable" states.[3]

What is now being suggested, and what was apparently intimated at the close of the earlier quotation from Bergson, is that this idea of an emergent development in the universe leads naturally to and is incomplete without, the further idea of immortality. Let us look at two of the great steps in the long process that has taken place. The first is the step from matter to life. This is a step up, for matter is inorganic and inert, but life has the capability of growth, change, and adaptation. It is a step to a new freedom. A rock lies in its place. The lowliest lichen that climbs upon its surface grows. Water lies stagnant, but the protozoa in it move, divide, and multiply. Furthermore, at the dividing point between matter and life there are foreshadowings of what is to come. In a great college devoted to scientific studies I once heard the dean of the graduate division deliver an address on the question, "How Small Can a Thing

Be, and Still Be Alive?" The point of his address was that at this dividing line between matter and life, it is very difficult to know exactly where to make the demarcation. It is hard to tell at precisely what place life begins. There is a foreshadowing at the line of what is to come.

Then there is the step from life to thought. This is a step up indeed. To live by instinct is one thing; to live by insight is another. Man enjoys the benefits of living on the level of existence where he can think. The step up from life to thought is a step to greater freedom. Du Noüy remarks that it has taken man but three generations to conquer the air, whereas it took the animals hundreds of thousands of years. Freedom is possible in one's own life because one can think, plan, and make a program for oneself, and carry it out to accomplishment. And at the dividing line, there is a certain foreshadowing of what is to come. Where, exactly, would you draw the line at which thought begins? Is it only man who is capable of thinking? Are there rudiments of the power of thought in animals? What about the dog that was observed on Eighteenth Avenue in Denver? Traffic is heavy both ways along that thoroughfare. This dog would frequently come to the street, and wish to cross. Standing on the curb, he would lift one foot and hold it in the air. Then he would hobble out into the street, and limp painfully across, while all the traffic drew to a halt to allow the poor crippled dog to pass. When he got across, the dog would put his fourth foot back down on the street and gallop off in his customary good spirits. Where does thinking begin?

Now, the theory here being suggested is that there is yet another step in the great universal process. Is it not ridiculous to suppose that the development thus far described has been brought through all these ages and throughout the vast expanses of this world, to the point of life and thought, and then is all to be cut off here? If the process ends abruptly at this point, what was the purpose of it after all? May we not therefore suppose that there is another step, and that having come up to life and thought, the next step is the step up to immortality?

That would be a step up indeed. It would presumably be a step into greater freedom. In this world we are obstructed by space and time, and there we might be in what one writer calls the unobstructed universe. There we would presumably be free from the materially restricting things of this present life, and from the hampering, crippling things of this present earthly tabernacle.

And at the dividing line we might expect that there would be some foreshadowings of what is to come. If the mind at its highest level has any ability to reach across space and time, that could be a possible foreshadowing of an ultimate transcendence of space and time. As a matter of fact, experiments in our day have been taken by many researchers to demonstrate the existence of such a power of the mind. If that is correct, then we have here the same thing which was found at the other dividing lines lower down the scale—a hint already of the transcendence and the greater freedom which will be exhibited in the higher level, which in this case is that of immortality.

BIBLE TEACHINGS AND THE RESURRECTION OF CHRIST

If the theory which has been outlined in the preceding paragraphs is correct at all, we live in a universe in which there is certainly room for immortality and in which, indeed, there are already indications that there is a level of existence beyond the present. Now we turn directly to the Bible to ask what is taught and told there concerning the resurrection.

At first we may be disappointed in this inquiry, because in the earlier portions of the Bible there is little or nothing said concerning life beyond. The blessing that is sought is length of days in the present life. But even at the time that the literary sources are speaking only of this life, we know from archeological discoveries that belief in something beyond death prevailed among the people. Many ancient Hebrew graves have been excavated, in which the body of the deceased was laid away with evident respect and care, and in which objects such as lamps, oil juglets, dishes, jars, jewelry, and knives were placed. As one writer says in surveying this evidence, "The implication is that death was not the end of the individual and that his soul would be benefited by the due respect to his body."[4]

When the Old Testament does speak of the beyond it most often makes reference to Sheol. Sheol was evidently thought of as a shadowy place in the underworld where the deceased experienced a wretched sort of half-life, and thus the conception evoked but little hopefulness in the minds of those who held it. It was like the Hades of the Greeks, of which Homer made the dead Achilles say:

> I would be
> A laborer on earth and serve for hire
> Some man of mean estate, who makes scant cheer,
> Rather than reign over all who have gone down
> To death.

Thus when Jacob thought that Joseph was dead, he said, "I shall go down to Sheol to my son, mourning." Hannah sang, "The Lord . . . brings down to Sheol." When Hezekiah recovered from sickness, he wrote:

> Thou hast held back my life
> from the pit of destruction.
> Sheol cannot thank thee,
> death cannot praise thee;
> those who go down to the pit cannot hope
> for thy faithfulness.

The Psalmist called the underworld "the land of forgetfulness." The prophet Isaiah described the descent of the king of Babylon to Sheol, and pictured the shades greeting him with the words, "You too have become as weak as we!"[5]

In a few Old Testament passages, generally held to be of a relatively late date, we find a doctrine of resurrection. Job asks tentatively, "If a man die, shall he live again?" Isaiah sings, "Thy dead shall live; their bodies shall rise." One Psalm expresses the hope, "Afterward thou wilt receive me to glory." And in Daniel it is written, "Many of those who sleep in the dust of the earth shall awake, some to everlasting life, and some to shame and everlasting contempt."[6] The belief thus expressed most clearly in Old Testament sources in Daniel, was accepted by the Pharisees, although denied by the Sadducees, and was probably generally held by the common people of the time of Jesus. It is reflected in the statement of Martha to Jesus about her deceased brother Lazarus, as recorded in John 11:24: "I know that he will rise again in the resurrection at the last day." From the tone of this remark and the behavior of all the mourners on this occasion it is evident that the belief was in such a distant event that it did little to mitigate the bitterness of the sorrow which was felt.

What was the teaching of Jesus? When he died on the cross, it is recorded that one of the other two men crucified at the same time, besought him, "Jesus, remember me when you come in your kingly power," and that Jesus said to him, "Truly, I say to you, today you will be with me in Paradise."[7] This statement does not suggest an interminable wait until a distant resurrection, but a swift crossing of the boundary between this life and the risen life beyond. Similarly the answer of Christ to Martha was, "I am the resurrection and the life; he who believes in me, though he die, yet shall he live, and whoever lives and believes in me shall never die."[8]

Likewise Paul—although in some passages he seems to share the common Jewish view of a more distant resurrection—when he finally faces the possibly imminent end of his own life, writes to his Philippian friends that "to depart and be with Christ . . . is far better."[9] And, as if it were a fact all the time but not previously well recognized, II Timothy 1:10 declares: "Our Savior Christ Jesus . . . brought life and immortality to light." Thus Lyman Abbott was doubtless justified in the affirmation: "Isolated and enigmatical texts cannot countervail the generic teaching which the New Testament emphasizes throughout, that a life personally in fellowship with the Lord Jesus Christ and nourished by him is always a life eternal; that the life of righteousness, unselfishness, and serviceableness never dies, never ceases to exist, but ever lives with an ever-increasing fullness."[10]

The New Testament not only contains this teaching about a continued and more glorious life after this life, but it also embodies the testimony of the earliest disciples of Jesus to the fact that he actually appeared to them alive after his own death. The oldest written statement of the evidence is in the fifteenth chapter of I Corinthians. There Paul names three individuals and three groups to whom Christ appeared. The first individual was Cephas or Peter whom Paul had visited in Jerusalem for fifteen days not long after his own conversion. Thus Paul doubtless had Peter's report first hand. Further, the two men could hardly have been in collusion to deceive the world, since on subjects where they did not agree Paul did not hesitate to oppose Peter to his face. The second individual was James. Paul also saw him on the same visit to Jerusalem, and also later pursued a separate course from his. This James was probably the brother of Jesus, and we know from John 7:5 that "his brothers did not believe in him." Hence it is not likely that James was predisposed to imagine a vision of Christ. The third was Paul himself, and thus we have the direct statement of one of those who saw him. Furthermore this was a man who had violently persecuted the early Christian movement.

The three groups to whom the risen Christ appeared were the twelve, more than five hundred brethren, and all the apostles. Of the more than five hundred, the majority were still alive when Paul wrote, and it sounds as if many were known to him personally. These groups can hardly have been the victims of mass psychology, since in that case we should have expected the experiences to spread to more and more, whereas here they are strictly limited. In fact, the members of the groups were poorly enough prepared to be subjects of mass delusion, since we find numerous references in the gospel accounts of the appearances to the doubts which they had. Indeed, in so far as they had been followers of Jesus already, they were at the time bitterly disappointed and thoroughly discouraged persons.

When the more detailed accounts of the appearances are perused in the Gospels it is made clear that the Jesus whom the disciples saw was recognizably the same person they had already known. He was a real person and living a real life. He was able to function in this world, walking on its roads and standing in its rooms. Yet he transcended this world and the ordinary limitations of space and time, and was living in a form of existence higher than the earthly.

Therefore the resurrection of Jesus is the demonstration and the foundation for the teaching concerning continued and more glorious life which is found in the New Testament, which we have also suggested is in harmony with what we know of the emergence of successively higher levels of being in the universe. Lyman Abbott even said: "The resurrection of Jesus Christ was not an extraordinary event; it was an extraordinary evidence of an ordinary event."[11] Surprising as this affirmation may seem at first sight, it is in fact quite in harmony with the statement of Paul in I Corinthians 15:22-23 when he says that "in Christ shall all be made alive," and that Christ himself is the "first fruits." As Christ was raised from the dead so shall others be. Life after death is a fact. But in the special case of Jesus Christ he was most amazingly made manifest to his disciples in the reality and transcendence of his risen life.

Pictures of the Transition

In the foregoing we have held, both in the light of science and of our religion, that death is really a transition from the terrestrial to the transcendent. When one endeavors to speak of this great change, it is of course necessary to use the language of parable or symbol. In the light of our analysis of the successive emergent levels of existence, it is appropriate to speak of death as commencement. When one graduates from school, whether it is high school or college, there is always a tinge of sadness about the conclusion of years which, in retrospect, appear more valuable and wonderful than ever. But the exercise that comes at the end of school is never called a program of ending. It has become customary to call it "commencement." And on the view set forth in this chapter, that is exactly what death would be. Ralph Sockman says, "The more I study the Gospels, the more I come to believe that we pass from this life to the next by way of a schoolroom rather than by way of a courtroom. Eternal life is the extension of the courses we take here.

God gives us another chance, but he does not change the rules of the school."[12]

In the New Testament other metaphors are used. Death is called sleep. "Our friend Lazarus has fallen asleep," said Jesus when he announced the death of the brother of Martha and Mary. When Stephen was stoned, "he fell asleep." The deceased at Thessalonica were "those who have fallen asleep."[13] When the early Christians referred to a burial ground they used the word *coemeterium,* which was found both in Greek and Latin and from which obviously the English word "cemetery" is derived. This word meant literally a sleeping chamber. But what happens when one falls asleep? One awakens again in the morning. Refreshed by rest, one picks up the thread of life and goes on again. Such is the suggestion of this term.

Departure is another term. At the time of his transfiguration, according to Luke 9:31, Jesus talked with his disciples and discussed with them the "departure which he was to accomplish at Jerusalem." Here the original Greek word is literally "exodus." In the exodus the children of Israel left the land of bondage and went out to the land of promise. That was wonderful. Even so, death is an exodus from a land in which there is much bondage to sin and sickness and sorrow, into a land of glorious promise. Also in II Timothy 4:6 death is spoken of as departure: "The time of my departure has come." Here, however, it is a different Greek word which is in the original text. This word literally means "unloosing for departure," and thus calls up the picture of the casting off of the moorings of a ship when it moves out to sea. Thus death is the casting off of the moorings of earthly life as the ship moves out to the eternal ocean.

Again, death is home going. According to John 14:2 Jesus said, "In my Father's house are many rooms." Here we dwell in one room of the Father's house. But this room, much as it is now home to us, does not exhaust the magnitude and the marvel of the Father's great house. And in that house there are other rooms. Dying is going on into another room. Since it is the Father's house, it is home going rather than going into a strange and fearsome place.

> Goin' home . . .
> Quietlike, some still day, I'm jes' goin' home.
> It's not far, jes' close by, through an open door.[14]

CHAPTER SEVENTEEN

How to Think About the Last Judgment

According to the theory of immortality and the doctrine of resurrection set forth in the preceding chapter, every human being will survive death and, beyond it, will experience a continuation of real personal existence upon a higher level than here. Does this then eliminate the thought of judgment? By no means. Rather, it shows more plainly than ever the inevitability and inexorability of judgment.

Phases of Judgment

That there is a judgment in the present life is, of course, unmistakable. When Paul says in Romans 1:18 that "the wrath of God is revealed from heaven against all ungodliness and wickedness of men," it is not his intention to describe an anthropomorphic deity of petulant mood but to point to the actual state of affairs in human life as evidence of the appalling results of sin. The deterioration of character and the corruption of society consequent upon evil-doing are sufficient evidence of the silent, ceaseless, and inescapable working of the divine judgment. The agony of a dope addict, the remorse of an unfaithful person, the callousness of one to whom the finer sentiments have ceased to make any appeal, the futile struggles to escape of one enmeshed by his own deed in a net of evil circumstances, the social consequences of the practice of slavery, the bitter aftermath for Western nations of their years of colonialism and exploitation in the East, and many, many more facts are witness of this judgment.

There is also a judgment in death itself. There is an irreversible finality about death. Earthly life is now ended. The sculptor's chisel is laid down, the artist's brush is put aside. What has been done has been done; what is undone will never be done. "The sting of death," Paul declares in I Corinthians 15:56, "is sin." That which makes death dreadful is the fact of sin. The deeds and the misdeeds of life have been completed. There is now no changing of a single thing. And this itself is judgment.

But is there also judgment in the life beyond? What does the Bible teach about this?

Bible Teachings

In the foregoing chapter it has been suggested, using an earthly illustration, that the passing from this life to the next is like graduation from school or college, an event for which we customarily use the term commencement. But every graduation involves a judgment, for records are kept, conditions have to be satisfied, degrees of honor may be assigned, and recommendations are made for the future. The completion of one stage of training is the indispensable prerequisite for progress in the next, and failure necessarily imposes a handicap with regard to what lies beyond. This general line of thought concerning the judgment is fully justified by the Bible and in particular by the import of the parable of the talents in the twenty-fifth chapter of the Gospel according to Matthew. "Well done, good and faithful servant; you have been faithful over a little, I will set you over much," is the commendation of the master to the servants who have used their talents effectively; but "take the talent from him, and give it to him who has the ten talents," is the decree with regard to the man who has done nothing with the talent entrusted to him.

The idea of separation is also involved in New Testament pictures of judgment. Weeds and wheat grow together in the same field, but at harvest the weeds are bound in bundles to be burned, the wheat is gathered into the barn. The net gathers fish of every kind, but when it is full men sort the good into vessels and throw away the bad. The shepherd separates the sheep from the goats, and places the sheep at his right hand, but the goats at the left.[1]

And repudiation, too, is mentioned. The Lord will say to many who profess to have worked for him, "I never knew you; depart from me, you evildoers."[2] Thus far, then, we may suppose that all do indeed survive death, but that in the further life not all are found fitted to be on the same level, in the same group, or in the same associations.

Next we find a number of pictures used relative to judgment, all of which carry the idea of revelation.

The judgment will consist in the revealing to us of how we really are. It will be like the wind blowing. Psalm 1:4-5 says: "The wicked . . . are like the chaff which the wind drives away. Therefore the wicked will not stand in the judgment." In his book *Of Men and Mountains,* William O. Douglas told of standing on Old Snowy, a mountain in the northwest, with the gale sweeping across it. He remembered the intrigue and double-dealing which he had encountered among men. He wrote:

> All that, I thought, is the froth of life that would disappear on the wings of the northwester on Old Snowy. It would be gone as quickly and as silently as a shout in this gale. The wind would whip away intrigue and scheming. It would clear the air of the vain boasts of men. The petty politician would stand naked; and in his nakedness his character would be revealed. The peddler of gossip would be deprived of his pen and his smirk; he would stand whimpering and friendless. Schemes would fall helplessly from men's lips on this rocky ridge. Man stands here as I imagine he stands on Judgment Day—naked and alone, judged by the harmony of his soul, by his spiritual strength, by the purity of his heart.[3]

Judgment will be like the light shining. This was the kind of judgment which Christ brought into the world, which will presumably be only less escapable in the beyond: "This is the judgment, that the light has come into the world, and men loved darkness rather than light, because their deeds were evil."[4] The poet writes:

> Eternal Light! Eternal Light!
> How pure that soul must be,
> When, placed within Thy searching sight,
> It shrinks not, but with calm delight
> Can live, and look on Thee.

O how shall I, whose native sphere
Is dark, whose mind is dim,
Before the Ineffable appear,
And on my naked spirit bear
The uncreated beam?[5]

It will be like the reading of the book, in which is the record of all one's deeds. "And I saw the dead, great and small, standing before the throne, and books were opened. . . . And the dead were judged by what was written in the books, by what they had done."[6] There is a short story by H. G. Wells entitled "A Vision of Judgment." In it the angel is pictured reading from the book. The wicked man who had been proud of how bad he was, listened to some of the things he had done and was so horribly ashamed of how silly they sounded and of how silly he had been, that he could not bear it. The saint, who had done so many unpleasant things in order to get to paradise, listened to the reading of the book, and it became plain that he had made a perfect nuisance of himself. And in turn, the writer too fled into the great sleeve of God as the inexorable reading went on.

The further conception of judgment, therefore, which we find suggested in biblical reference, is that of realization. When things are made unmistakably plain, there will come realization. In Revelation 1:7 we read that "he is coming . . . and every eye will see him, every one who pierced him; and all tribes of the earth will wail on account of him." What more severe judgment is there than to really see the wounds we have caused? G. A. Studdert-Kennedy somewhere tells the story of a drunken man who used to beat his little boy. One day the lad was lying on his cot very ill, and the father, sober for once, was leaning over him. In delirium the little boy held his hands in front of his face and cried, "Don't let him hit me, Mummy." For the first time the father realized what he had been doing. Charles William Stubbs wrote about conscience and future judgment:

> The ghost of forgotten actions
> Came floating before my sight,
> And things that I thought were dead things
> Were alive with a terrible might;
> And the vision of all my past life
> Was an awful thing to face,
> Alone with my conscience sitting
> In that solemn silent place.
> And I know of the future Judgment,
> How dreadful soe'er it be,
> To sit alone with my conscience
> Will be judgment enough for me.[7]

And Whittier penned the lines:

> Still shall the soul around it call
> The shadows which it gathered here,
> And painted on the eternal wall,
> The Past shall reappear.

As far as we have been able to see, therefore, judgment is inevitable and inexorable in this life, in the moment of death, and in the beyond. It consists in our being put with what we have fitted ourselves for, in having the true nature of ourselves made wholly plain, and in being brought to a realization of what we have done. Studdert-Kennedy has put it like this:

> The Day of Judgment is to me not so much an act in time as a process in eternity. That tremendous picture . . . of the Judgment Throne, with all the nations of the world gathered before

it, is to me . . . a picture of today and tomorrow and the beyond. . . .

A man lives a life of quite ordinary immorality . . . as his companions live; and then one day he gathers up into his arms a little baby born blind, and knows that he struck out its eyes. . . .

For a century the life of Europe rolled on, with . . . its tyrannies and oppressions . . . its idiotic trust in force . . . and then came the Day of Judgment. In the flashlight of a million guns, in the groans of dying men and the wailing of countless widows, in the agony and bloody sweat of a continent racked with pain, we were made to see whither we had been going, and what it meant. . . .

Because as each day of judgment reveals the meaning of all other days that have preceded it, and sums up in a flash the history of a man or the history of a continent, so it seems to me that some day there must come a great Judgment Day, a great crisis, which will sum up the meaning of all history, from its strange beginning to its far-off and inconceivable end—a great day when the meaning of every evil thing shall be finally revealed, and in that flash of revelation perish and come to an end. . . . From that day a new and wonderful movement must begin, the movement of pure goodness, untainted by evil, toward the beatific Vision and the splendour of His Face.[8]

The Purpose of Judgment

The question which remains to be asked is as to the purpose of judgment. In the last analysis this question must be answered upon the basis of our understanding of the nature of God and of Jesus Christ. According to Christian faith, the nature of God is that of the Father, and the nature of Jesus Christ is that of the Savior. Therefore the judgment which takes place according to God's arrangement of his universe, and in which we meet him in whom is the light which judges all men, must be intended for salvation. It cannot be the purpose of the God whom Jesus called the Father in heaven, to punish men uselessly. The punishment which is involved in judgment must be intended to work for the redemption of men.

As for the picture of the lake of fire into which, according to Revelation 20:15, those are thrown whose names are not found written in the book of life, is it not the function of fire to consume all rubbish but to refine any precious metal? And when the fire is called "eternal," the Greek word is literally "aeonian," which means lasting for an aeon or an age. If it meant "endless," we would have to agree with Leslie D. Weatherhead that the phrase would be self-contradictory. "Punishment," writes Weatherhead, "is a concept that implies making the wrongdoer a rightdoer. . . . If hell is endless, it is valueless. . . . Suffering from which nothing can be learned, nothing gained, is meaningless, and he who inflicted it would be a fiend, not a father."[9]

Finally, we may be sure that it will always be the purpose of Jesus Christ "to seek and to save the lost."[10] As Weatherhead says, "Christ, that great Seeker of souls and Believer in men, will never sit down contented on the throne of his glory if there is one coin bearing the image and superscription of the King lying in the dust of evil, if any seeking on his part can restore it. And that great Shepherd of the sheep, who cannot bear the thought of a one per cent loss, will never abandon his search if there is one sheep still capable of hearing his voice and responding to it, out on the cold, dark mountains, helpless, hopeless, and alone."[11]

PART THREE

THE CHURCH

CHAPTER EIGHTEEN

The Intention of Jesus for the Church

Did Jesus intend to found the church? There are those who answer that of course he did, and not only that, but he appointed an individual man to be the head of the church. This was Peter, and Jesus expected the successors of that man to be the heads of it down through all time.

There are others, and among them are many modern scholars, who say that Jesus did not intend at all to found a church. The word church, they observe, occurs in only two places in the Gospels, in Matthew 16:18 and Matthew 18:17, and it may very well be that in these passages the later Christians put in a word which Jesus himself did not even use. What he talked about, these scholars point out, was the kingdom of God. What he believed, they say, was that this was going to come very soon, and consequently there was no place and no time for a church to be established. We will therefore have to investigate the question for ourselves, and try to find out what we can about Jesus' intention.

A New Group

For one thing, it seems evident that Jesus definitely intended to call together a new group of people. He himself belonged to the Jewish people. According to the Scriptures they had a special place in God's plan, yet the same Scriptures contained the words of the prophets who declared that they had failed and that something new would have to come to pass. As described in the Old Testament, one distinguishing mark of the Jewish people was that they had been organized in twelve tribes. This organization reflected their early nomadic background, but was preserved even when they became a highly civilized kingdom, as in the time of Solomon, and was never forgotten. In view of this fact it can hardly be accidental that Jesus selected twelve men to be his closest associates and the leaders in his work. The word "church" may not appear often in the Gospels, but all the Gospels refer to "the twelve" whom Jesus appointed. Matthew, Mark, and Luke, all give lists of the names of these twelve men. In some cases we know, after that, almost nothing about them, but since they were the twelve whom Jesus picked, their names were carefully preserved. Luke 6:12 states that Jesus prayed all night long before he selected these men. John 6:70 records the emphatic question, "Did I not choose you?" According to John 15:16 he said to them, "You did not choose me, but I chose you." It was not accidental that Jesus picked a group of twelve men to lead his movement. There is some reflection here of the twelve tribes of Israel and some thought of a new group in which God's purpose will be worked out.

Another distinguishing mark of the Jewish people was their covenant with their God. The following characteristics of that covenant are set forth in the Old Testament: It was made between God and man at Mount Sinai, under the leadership of Moses. It was based upon commandments, especially the ten commandments. These were written on tables of stone, which is exactly the way important documents were inscribed in ancient times. The covenant was ratified with the blood of animals. Oxen were slain, and the blood of these sacrificed animals was sprinkled upon the altar at the foot of Mount Sinai. The covenant required obedience; it had to be kept if God were to give his blessing. It wrought fear, for Exodus 20:18 tells how "the people were afraid and trembled; and they stood afar off." The covenant was limited within rather narrow boundaries, for it was intended for a particular people. Finally it failed, as the prophets declared, because the people did not live up to all that it required.

Again, it cannot be an accident that Jesus speaks about a new covenant, as he is recorded to have done at the Last Supper.[1] There must be some backward look here to the former covenant, and some thought of the institution of a new agreement between God and the group gathered around Jesus. Comparing this covenant with the former one, the following points may be observed: It was an agreement between God and man, made in an upper room under the leadership of Jesus. It was based, not upon commandments, but upon principles, for that was what was emphasized in the teaching of Jesus. These principles were not written on tablets of stone, which after all one could throw down and break, as Moses once did when he became disgusted with what his people were doing, but were written upon the hearts of men, as an ancient prophet had said would be the case in the future: "I will write it upon their hearts."[2] This new agreement was ratified, not by the slaying of sacrificial animals as in the past, but by the blood of Christ himself. It called not so much for obedience, which man some way never can render perfectly and fully, but for faith, an attitude of loving trust in God. It did not work out into fear, but rather into love. It was not limited to the narrow boundaries which prevailed in the past, for Jesus expressed the expectation that many would come from east and west and sit at table with Abraham, Isaac, and Jacob in the kingdom of God.[3]

In these two facts, therefore, to which the Gospels bear witness, that Jesus appointed twelve leaders and that he spoke about a new covenant, there is evidence that it was his intention to call into being a group of people which had a relationship to the group with which God had been working but which had possibilities beyond those which had been realized in the past. Whether or not he himself used the word "church" to describe the group can perhaps not be determined for sure, but seems by no means unlikely since it is the same as the word "assembly," which is frequently used in the Old Testament for the community or congregation of Israel, particularly when gathered together for a holy purpose.[4]

A New Program

We may also observe that Jesus actually started a new program. This program had as its distinguishing marks a ceremony of introduction and a ceremony of fellowship. These will be discussed more fully in later chapters of this book but must at least be mentioned at this point. The ceremony of introduction was that of baptism. Jesus himself was baptized at the beginning of his work by John the Baptist in the Jordan River. According to the Fourth Gospel, those who became followers of Jesus were taken into the new relationship by the same sort of ceremony. John 3:22 states of Jesus and his disciples that "he remained with them and baptized." John 4:2 explains that "Jesus himself did not baptize, but only his disciples." This provides the understandable sequence which leads to the practice of the early church, where we find baptism taken for granted as the usual way of entrance into the Christian movement.

The ceremony of association was that of eating together. Already during the course of his ministry, Jesus and his disciples must often have broken bread together. The observance of a religious fellowship meal, known as the *haburah,* was a practice among other Jewish groups at the time, and the meals of Jesus and his disciples may even have been somewhat like that observance. At any meal it is probable that the leader would consecrate the bread and the cup with a blessing at the beginning. Finally, when Jesus ate for the very last time with the twelve, he spoke to them with special solemnity and brought the bread and cup into connection with his own death. So the common meal was never forgotten, and was an observance of the early church.

The new program also involved the proclamation of a message. This message was about the kingdom of God, for which the Jewish people had long hoped and which had now drawn near in a special way. Indeed, the kingdom was already present in the presence and work of Jesus, yet was to grow like a plant springing up from a seed, and was finally to come in a wonderful and climactic way. To speak about the kingdom of God was also to have to speak about God himself, and the new message was that God is the Father, who loves and cares for every individual. The kingdom has to do with men, too, and here the message was that men are brothers and bound to love one another. Summed up, the message was embodied in two commandments both of which were to be found in the Old Testament but which were combined now in a way which was at once self-evidently correct and at the same time startling in simplicity: "Love God; love your neighbor as yourself."[5]

Furthermore, the program called men to a mission. As stated in Mark 3:14-15 the task of the twelve leaders, and ideally therefore of all of Jesus' followers, was threefold. First, he called these men "to be with him," so that they might learn from him. Second, they were "to be sent out to preach," so that they might go out and tell the good news to others. Third, they were to "have authority to cast out demons," that is to minister for the healing of the disorders of mankind. No better description is needed than this of the mission of the church; people are to gather and be with

Christ; they are to preach and tell about him; they are to serve for the healing of the ills and the woes of the world.

A New Promise

Jesus not only called into being a new group of people, and gave them a new program, but he also gave them a new promise. For one thing, he promised to his followers persecution. "If they have called the master of the house Beelzebul, how much more will they malign those of his household." "Blessed are you when men revile you and persecute you and utter all kinds of evil against you falsely on my account . . . so men persecuted the prophets who were before you."[6] But he also promised them power and victory. "Fear not, little flock," he said, "for it is your Father's good pleasure to give you the kingdom." "I will build my church, and the powers of death shall not prevail against it."[7]

Now if he spoke such words as these to his followers, it seems evident that he expected them to constitute a movement which would continue, which would encounter opposition, and which would ultimately prevail. This was an expectation for the ongoing of his church. It was, therefore, the intention of Jesus that a group of people—as many as would, both within the limits of Judaism and from outside—should be called together into a new covenant with God; that they should go on a mission into the world to proclaim the message of God's kingdom; and that they should have the power to endure persecution and win the victory.

CHAPTER NINETEEN

What Happened at Pentecost?

There was in a sense an anticipation of the church in the holy congregation of the Old Testament, there was certainly a nucleus of it in the gathering of the disciples around Jesus, but according to the book of Acts there was a special event which transpired on the day of Pentecost and which marked a decisive moment in the origins of the church. Indeed, it is not too much to say that, according to Acts, the church began on the day of Pentecost. We must therefore ask what happened at that time?

THE PROBLEM OF PENTECOST

From the prominence it is given in the New Testament, it might be expected that Pentecost would rank as a church anniversary second only to Christmas and Easter, but it is doubtful if it plays so large a role in the thinking of most of the churches today. Indeed many people trained in modern ways of thought would probably admit that to them Pentecost is more of an enigma than an inspiration.

In trying to understand the meaning of Pentecost we can at any rate begin with the fact that at that time an ordinary Jewish feast was observed. In the course of the year the Jewish people celebrated a series of festivals which were high points in the observance of their religion. One of these was Passover, which is relatively well known to most readers of the Bible and which will be mentioned again in another chapter in this book. After Passover, later in the spring came the festival of Pentecost. It occurred at the time of the wheat harvest in Palestine, hence was known as the Feast of Harvest. At that time the people remembered how God had shown Noah the rainbow in the sky, after the great flood, and had promised him that seedtime and harvest would always continue. They also believed that God had given the law to Moses at Mount Sinai at this same time of year, so they celebrated that event too in the festival. When the feast was placed at an exact point in the calendar it was put fifty days after Passover. As the law of the feast is stated in Leviticus 23:15-16: "You shall count from the morrow after the sabbath [of the Passover] . . . seven full weeks . . . counting fifty days to the morrow after the seventh sabbath." Since the feast fell on the fiftieth day it was often simply called by that name, and that is what Pentecost means—"fiftieth." The day after the sabbath is of course the first day of the week or, as we call it today, Sunday. In A.D. 30, Pentecost Sunday fell on a date equivalent to our May 28.

At the time, then, that an ordinary Jewish feast took place, an extraordinary event transpired among the followers of Jesus. These persons were assembled in a house in Jerusalem and this is what Acts 2:2-4 says took place: "And suddenly a sound came from heaven like the rush of a mighty wind, and it filled all the house where they were sitting. And there appeared to them tongues as of fire, distributed and resting on each one of them. And they were all filled with the Holy Spirit and began to speak in other tongues, as the Spirit gave them utterance." It is further reported that many people from different nations were present at Jerusalem at that time, and that when they saw what happened they asked, "What does this mean?" That is exactly the question we are asking now.

In attempting to answer this question, one line of thought runs somewhat as follows. The book of Acts tells in its conclusion about Paul's two years in custody in Rome, which must have been at a date as late as A.D. 60. Therefore the book of Acts cannot have been written until after A.D. 60, and it may be that a more probable date is around A.D. 90. The book was written, accordingly, from thirty to sixty years after the date of the Pentecost event. In the later part of the book of Acts, excerpts from the diary of a travel companion of Paul are found which provide very detailed and evidently reliable information about the happenings with which they deal. But for the early part of the book the author had to depend upon stories which had been handed down for many years and had been much embellished in repeated retellings. The proof that this is the case is that these stories narrate miraculous events which naturally did not really happen. Perhaps the account of Pentecost was even invented by the author of Acts to provide an occasion parallel to the giving of the Law at Mount Sinai as the foundation occurrence of the Christian church. At any rate, what we have in the second chapter of the book of Acts is a late, legendary story about an event of the distant past, the exact nature of which can no longer be recovered. Possibly, we may suppose, the followers of Jesus had a specially impressive prayer meeting, felt specially inspired, and this story grew up about it. The foregoing view is substantially that held, with variations, by many modern scholars, and it may be essentially correct.

Others, however, believe that on the day of Pentecost a very remarkable, unique, miraculous event took place. To them it seems appropriate that on the occasion of the launching of the Christian church God should disregard the ordinary laws of nature and cause certain amazing happenings to transpire. The founding of the church was a once-for-all event; it was not surprising that once-for-all phenomena took place at the same time.

Yet another possible view is that the event did take place on the day of Pentecost just as it is recorded in the book of Acts, and that this is only a remarkable example of what can happen when men come in contact with higher spiritual levels of the universe. The chief phenomena of Pentecost were the sound like the rush of a mighty wind, the tongues as of fire resting on each person, and the speaking of words intelligible to persons of different native languages. In reports of their experiences both Stewart Edward White and Anice Terhune refer to something like the blowing of a draft of cold air.[1] William Crookes, later president of the British Association for the Advancement of Science, told of seeing luminous points of light which darted about and settled on the heads of different persons.[2] Leslie D. Weatherhead attests the ability of an uneducated coal miner to speak for a time under certain circumstances in the perfect diction and accent of an Oxford scholar,[3] while there are records of others who even spoke in languages normally unknown to them.[4] While the evidences in such areas as have just been alluded to are still subject to many questions, enough data have already been attested by persons thoroughly scientific in the spirit of their investigations, to make it seem obligatory to keep an open mind on the subject and to raise the suggestion that at some time in the future the phenomena recorded in the second chapter of Acts will be set in the light of a reasonable theory of man's relationship to spiritual realities.

The Preparation for Pentecost

Granted, then, that the early followers of Jesus experienced an assemblage of remarkable importance on the day of Pentecost and that the day was afterward remembered as in a real sense the birthday of the church, we have next to ask what happened to lead up to that event?

For one thing, Acts 2:1 tells us that at that time the followers of Jesus "were all together in one place." According to Acts 1:15 there were about 120 followers of Jesus at that time, and if all these were included it was a meeting of considerable size. The house where they met may have been the same as that to which Peter came when he was released from prison as recorded in Acts 12:12, namely the house of Mary the mother of John Mark. Elsewhere in the New Testament there are numerous references to the meetings of the early Christians in the homes of members, and presumably it was often those who had commodious houses who thus made them available. It was in a common place, then, and doubtless also with a unity of spirit that the followers of Jesus were assembled in Jerusalem on the day of Pentecost. As the King James Version puts it: "They were all with one accord in one place." In such circumstances one of the promises of Christ could be fulfilled: "If two of you agree on earth about anything they ask, it will be done for them by my Father in heaven. For where two or three are gathered in my name, there am I in the midst of them."[5]

The prayer of the early followers of Jesus was as much a part of their preparation for Pentecost as their togetherness. According to the book of Acts the risen Christ showed himself to his disciples for forty days after his resurrection and then appeared to them in such a way that they knew that his continued appearances were no longer to be expected. After that, ten days remained until this Pentecost feast. The record in Acts 1:14 concerning the activity of Jesus' closest followers in this period states: "All these with one accord devoted themselves to prayer." This was also in line with what Jesus had already told them to do. To bring out the suggestion of continuing action in the Greek verb, Matthew 7:7-8 may properly be translated: "Keep on asking, and it will be given you; keep on seeking, and you will find; keep on knocking, and it will be opened to you. For every one who keeps on asking, receives, and he who keeps on seeking, finds, and to him who keeps on knocking, it will be opened."

Thus two things fundamentally constituted the preparation for Pentecost: togetherness in place and spirit, and continuance in prayer. It would seem that these are abiding prerequisites for the progress of the church.

The Power of Pentecost

What happened as a result of the experience at Pentecost? The power of the Holy Spirit was manifested at that time. Remembering earlier portions of this book and trying to put a profound doctrine into our own words, we may say something like this: When we look at the vast and wonderful world, we do not believe it could all have happened by accident. We do believe that there is a Creator, and it seems appropriate to speak of God the Creator as the Father. Then we look at history and see the life of Jesus. There is no life to compare with it anywhere through the centuries, or around all the lands of the earth. In his life we see the best that we know about God. In him we find a revelation of the nature and will of God. Therefore we speak about him as the Son of God. But even though God is invisible and the human life of Jesus ended long ago, we cannot help seeing and feeling that the influence of God and the influence of Christ still work in the world. Therefore with reference to this present, effective power we speak of the Holy Spirit. It was the power of the Holy Spirit which was manifested in the experience of the disciples.

Through the Holy Spirit the disciples received power at that time to persuade others. A great crowd came together, Peter stood up and told them about Jesus, and about three thousand persons believed what they heard and were baptized.

Power for missionary work also became effective. From that day the church began to spread through many lands. At Jerusalem on that day were people from many countries. The list of nationalities and lands sweeps from east to west: Parthians, Medes, Elamites, residents of Mesopotamia—these were from regions called Iran and Iraq today; then Judea is mentioned—right there in Palestine; after that Cappadocia, Pontus, Asia, Phrygia, and Pamphylia—these were provinces in what we call Asia Minor; then down across the sea—Egypt, and parts of Libya belonging to Cyrene; then Rome; and finally, almost as if in a miscellaneous category, Cretes and Arabians. Men were there from all over, and they must also have gone from there to all over the world because Christianity spread into these many places. Take Rome for example. The most reasonable explanation for the founding of the Christian church at Rome is that people from Rome who were in Jerusalem on the day of Pentecost, went back to Rome, told the message, and started the church. Peter probably reached Rome only later; Paul certainly had not been there yet when he wrote his letter to the Roman church. It must have been some of those nameless Christians who became followers of Christ at Pentecost in Jerusalem, and were inspired to carry the Christian message wherever they went, that account for the rise of the great church at Rome, and the Christian church in many other places around the world.

Has this ever happened again? Yes, it has happened

many times. In 1806, for example, a number of students at Williams College were talking about religion, were studying the Christian faith, and were praying. Several of them were out on a hike one day. A sudden thunderstorm came up and they took shelter in the lee of a haystack out in a field. There they continued to talk and to pray. They became the famous "Haystack Band," of which Samuel J. Mills was the leader, out of which the American Board of Commissioners for Foreign Missions of the Congregational church came into being, and from whose number Adoniram Judson went to Burma to found the great missionary work of the Baptist church in that land. Here, for most practical purposes, the same thing happened as at Pentecost. The prerequisites were the same: togetherness of believers, and prayer; and the results were the same: power to work, power to spread the gospel. Thus what happened at Pentecost can, at least in its most important elements, continue to happen in the church.

CHAPTER TWENTY

The Essential Nature of the Church

The Christian church which began so long ago with so few people, has spread and grown ever since. Today it exists in virtually every nation in the world, and is estimated to number more than 775 million members, about one-third of the total population of the world. It has far more adherents than any other single religion, although all of the non-Christian religions together are of course much more numerous. More than 160 different denominations and churches in more than forty countries now belong to the World Council of Churches. In the United States of America, the 1955 *Yearbook of American Churches* listed 255 religious bodies with a total membership of 94,842,845 persons, over 59.5 per cent of the population. In general these figures represent Christian churches and members, although they include a few groups which are outside of Christianity, such as Buddhists, Jewish congregations, and Mormons. The company of the followers of Christ is thus very numerous but also much divided. The different churches bear different names and vary from one another in many aspects of organization and life. The question is therefore raised as to what is the essential nature of the church?

The Traditional Churches

In general, the churches may be classified in two very large divisions. These are, first, the "traditional" churches; and, second, the "reformed" churches. The traditional churches are those which claim to have maintained a visible continuity from the earliest Christian church to the present. This continuity is to be seen in such things as the form of organization, the succession of authority, and the creedal statements. It is usually held that the organization of the church was definitely instituted by Christ and his apostles, and that spiritual authority has been handed down from them ever since through a succession of leaders in a traceable and unbroken line.

The Roman Catholic church claims to maintain this tradition. It takes literally the words of Jesus to Peter in Matthew 16:18: "You are Peter, and on this rock I will build my church. . . . I will give you the keys of the kingdom of heaven, and whatever you bind on earth shall be bound in heaven, and whatever you loose on earth shall be loosed in heaven." It holds that these words were addressed to Peter, not as a representative man of faith, but as the individual chosen to head the church. His possession of the keys is understood to mean that he has the authority to admit into the church and to exclude from it. In the version of the New Testament edited by the Confraternity of Christian Doctrine of the Roman Catholic church, the note to this passage explains about Peter: "He has complete power within the Church. . . . In heaven God ratifies the decisions which Peter makes on earth, in the name of Christ." It is also said that Peter went from Jerusalem to Rome where he served as the head of the church. There he was martyred and buried in the district known as the Vatican, where today stand the Church of St. Peter and the world headquarters of the Roman Catholic organization.

It is further believed that before he died, Peter ordained Linus, Cletus, and Clement to carry on after him. According to the *Book of the Popes,* compiled in the seventh century from earlier sources, Peter said to Clement: "As unto me was delivered by my Lord Jesus Christ the power to govern and to bind and loose, so also I commit unto thee, that thou mayest ordain stewards over divers matters who will carry onward the work of the church." Thereafter the records of the Roman Catholic church continue with a list of the names of nearly three hundred men who have exercised in succession the chief authority, down to the present Pope Pius XII who came to the papal throne in 1939. As the head of the church he bears the titles of Vicar of Christ, Successor of St. Peter, Bishop of Rome, Archbishop and Metropolitan of the Roman Province, Primate of Italy, Patriarch of the West, and Supreme Pontiff of the Universal Church. The theory of the authority of the pope as the direct successor of Peter was stated most plainly at the last general council of the Roman Catholic church at the Vatican in 1870:

> All the faithful of Christ must believe that the holy apostolic see and the Roman pontiff possesses the primacy over the whole world, and that the Roman pontiff is the successor of blessed

> Peter, prince of the apostles, and is true vicar of Christ and head of the whole Church . . . and that full power was given to him in blessed Peter to rule, feed, and govern the universal Church.

The same decree continues to explain that when the pope speaks in his official capacity to define a doctrine of faith or morals he is infallible.

The Eastern Orthodox churches also believe that they preserve a continuity of structure with the earliest church. By A.D. 451, in addition to the ecclesiastical authority of Rome which was recognized in the West, there were patriarchates at Constantinople, Alexandria, Antioch, and Jerusalem, each of which exercised authority over its surrounding region. These and yet other churches which were derived from them, such as the Ethiopian and Russian, were not too willing to accept the increasing claims of Rome to world supremacy. Growing disagreement and rivalry led at last to the Great Schism. In A.D. 1054 Pope Leo IX of Rome sent an embassy to deal with Patriarch Michael Cerularius of Constantinople. While the ambassadors were in Constantinople, the pope died. Cerularius thereupon declared that they had no authority. They in turn decided to break off relations. They marched into the splendid church of Hagia Sophia and deposited a bull of excommunication on the altar which condemned Cerularius and his adherents "along with all heretics, together with the devil and his angels." Cerularius was quite unperturbed, and thought indeed that he had won a personal victory. But the break between East and West was irreparable, and henceforth the various churches of the East went their own way. But since it was held that in each the ecclesiastical authorities had already been properly appointed in succession from the apostles, and that in each the true faith was truly preserved, it was believed that the Christian tradition was maintained unbroken.

For another example we may refer to a body which on many grounds belongs to the reformed churches, but which still attaches great weight to continuity of tradition and claims to maintain the apostolic authority in unbroken line. This is the Church of England and, in the United States of America, the Protestant Episcopal church. In A.D. 1534 the king of England, Henry VIII, broke with the Roman pope and by the Supremacy Act of Parliament became the "Supreme Head of the Church of England." For practical purposes this put him in the place of the pope for the English church, but the spiritual authority was still thought of as residing in the archbishop of Canterbury. In 1559 it became necessary to consecrate a new archbishop of Canterbury. Four men who had been ordained bishops earlier, laid hands on Matthew Parker and consecrated him to the position. Thus it was held by the English church that the apostolic succession was validly maintained. The Roman church, in 1896, declared the succession invalid, but the Anglican church has of course continued to affirm the validity of the apostolic succession which they preserve and to hold that it is of great importance.

The value of the emphasis upon tradition which we have been describing may be freely admitted. It has resulted in the maintaining in the churches of this type of at least a relatively large degree of unity and stability. But the danger in it must also be noted.

To define Christianity in terms of continuity of structure and leadership, makes the transmission of Christianity a formal act. If the hands of the right person are laid in the right way upon another person, spiritual authority is transmitted and the church continues to exist. But what if a copy of the New Testament in their language washed up on a hitherto unvisited island and the natives read it and believed it? What if they began to live as Christians, and to meet together and do things together as the early Christians did? Would the church not in fact exist there? Would it have to wait upon the arrival of a duly appointed dignitary from afar, who in turn would then appoint a leader and invest him with apostolic authority? If the natives were thinking and doing such things as the apostles did, would they not already be an apostolic church?

Likewise the traditional church may be betrayed into a false sense of security and self-satisfaction. If spiritual authority has indeed been transmitted to it, and it is the custodian of the keys of the kingdom of heaven, then it appears to enjoy an autonomy in the spiritual realm which is beyond criticism. Its properly ordained ministers constitute a special class of persons; its pronouncements have an unassailable validity; it is a law unto itself. If it becomes corrupt there is no point outside itself from which it can be criticized and corrected. This is, as a matter of fact, what happened in the case of the Roman Catholic church, and this is why in the Protestant Reformation another understanding of the nature of the church arose.

The Reformed Churches

The reformed churches constitute the second major division of Christendom. When corruption crept into the Roman Catholic church, Martin Luther and other reformers protested against it. Since by its basic theory that church was a norm unto itself, they could not appeal to it against itself. They had to find a norm outside of the church and independent of it, and this they found in the Bible. The Protestant Reformation both consisted in and grew out of a return to the Bible. The reformers validated their protest against the autonomous ecclesiastical structure in which grave abuses existed by appealing to the Bible, and they sustained their objection to what the duly appointed leaders of the organization were doing by appealing to the right, which the Bible justified, of every Christian to make his own response in faith directly to God and thus to be subservient to none.

Accordingly, all the many different denominations which eventually arose out of the movement were in some sense reformed. They were in one way or another attempts to re-establish the church as it was before it became corrupted, and in one sense or another they were restorations of the order of things which was attested, as they understood it, in the Bible. And, accordingly, all these denominations shared to some extent an understanding of the nature of the church which was fundamentally different from that of the traditional churches. To them, the essence of the church does not consist in the continuity of structure but in the continuity of biblical faith. The existence of an organization and a leadership which can be demonstrated to have come down across the centuries from the first apostles without a break, is not so important as the existence of a group of people who live by and make known in the world the same faith which the apostles had.

This return to the Bible included a return to the biblical proclamation. Jesus Christ presented his message of the kingdom of God in his words and acts, including his baptism and the last supper with the disciples. The apostles continued to tell about him through preaching and the observance of the ceremonies of baptism and the common meal. It is, therefore, wherever the message of Christ and about Christ is set forth in word and the ordinances, and is accepted, that the church exists. Martin Luther said:

> Wherever you see this Word preached, believed, confessed, and acted on, there do not doubt that there must be a true *ecclesia sancta catholica* [holy catholic church] . . . for God's word does not go away empty.

John Calvin declared:

> Wherever we see the word of God sincerely preached and heard, wherever we see the sacraments administered according to the institution of Christ, there we cannot have any doubt that the Church of God has some existence, since his promise cannot fail, "Where two or three are gathered together in my name, there am I in the midst of them."

The return to the Bible could involve going back not only to what was said in the Bible but also to what was done. The traditional churches are right in being concerned about how the church is organized and what its practices are, but the way to have right organization and practice is simply to go back to the beginning and do what was done at the first. Congregationalists hold that the church consists of local congregations like those of which the New Testament tells, made up of members who belong by their own free choice and who freely choose their own officers, one church being in no wise subservient to another but all being bound by the demands of Christian love to be helpful to each other. Baptists consider that their form of church organization reproduces the essentials of New Testament practice, and in particular believe that their usage and interpretation in regard to baptism are the same as in New Testament times. Disciples of Christ make a plea for the restoration of New Testament Christianity and think that the independence of the local congregation and the practice of baptism by immersion are important characteristics of the New Testament church.

The return to the Bible could also be interpreted as a return to biblical experience. Some have felt that what matters most is the experience of God which Jesus had and shared with his followers or, to use different language, the experience of the Holy Spirit which was given to the early church. Wherever such experience is found, they would maintain, regardless of how it is propagated, nourished, or expressed, there the true church exists in its essence. This way of thought has appealed to and been expressed by Protestant groups of great diversity. Pentecostal and Holiness bodies believe that where the Holy Spirit is recognizably present with power, there is the church.

The Society of Friends follows its founder, George Fox, in belief in the inner light, rejection of any professional ministry, and interpretation of the sacraments as inward and spiritual verities. On this view the Scriptures themselves cease to be of primary importance since the Spirit which inspired them can speak directly within the soul of every man. As Fox said to Margaret Fell: "What had any to do with the Scriptures, but as they came to the Spirit that gave them forth? You will say, Christ saith this, and the apostles this; but what canst thou say?" The Unitarian and Universalist churches use in their Orders of Service a prayer which expresses the conviction that it is the reproduction of the life of the spirit which matters in the church and that many inspiring examples of this life can be found in the past:

> In this house of remembrance, where we gather to meditate upon the life of the spirit, let us call to mind the great and the good who have blessed our race; the patient searchers after knowledge, the prophets of righteousness, the saints whose goodly lives shine across the ages, the humble folk whose names are forgotten but whose faithfulness was not in vain. While we give thanks that such as these have been, let us also strive to live in their spirit, and rejoice that in the generations to come souls no less noble will arise to yet greater heights of service and of love.

Thus the return to the Bible has been characteristic of the reformed churches as a whole, but among them there have been varying degrees of emphasis respectively upon the doctrine or the practice or the experience attested in the Bible. As a matter of fact, at each point the reformed churches have found occasion for division among themselves. Belief in the right of each to read and understand the Bible for himself has set each free to go in his own direction. Emphasis upon doctrine has led to the writing of various creeds, and these have become distinguishing marks of separate communions. Interest in the restoration of New Testament practice has resulted in the almost arbitrary selection of certain features found in New Testament churches, to the neglect of others, with the consequent result that what is confidently set forth by its proponents as a re-establishment of the New Testament church is judged by many other followers of Christ to be less than a complete embodiment of the richness of the Christian heritage. And the emphasis upon experience has led on the one hand to what has been called ardor without order,[1] and on the other to such a broad interpretation of spiritual experience that it is difficult to see in what wise the church differs from a humanistic society of self-culture.

Thus while the traditional churches, with their emphasis upon continuity of structure, fell into abuses but at least maintained a relatively large degree of unity within themselves, the reformed churches, with their emphasis upon continuity of biblical faith, accomplished a greatly needed renewal of church life, but found themselves going farther and farther apart until the result was the appalling diversity characteristic of Protestantism today. Therefore it is necessary to examine the New Testament again to see if there is not yet more guidance to be found there which will enable all the churches today to find their way forward and toward each other.

The New Testament Church

It must freely be admitted that the picture which the New Testament supplies of the church of that time does not provide a full and faultless pattern for the church today. Much that we would like to know about the church of the New Testament period is not told. Much that is told makes our problem difficult rather than easy. The churches which are described in the pages of the New Testament were not perfect. Their members were imperfect human beings and included Ananias and Sapphira at Jerusalem who practiced deceit, Euodia and Syntyche at Philippi who did not agree, and some at Corinth who became drunken at the common meal. Of seven churches to which letters are addressed in Revelation, two are praised, Smyrna the persecuted church, and Philadelphia the missionary church; but three are criticized, Ephesus the backsliding church, Pergamum the tolerant church, and Thyatira the compromising church; and two are condemned, Sardis the dead church, and Laodicea the lukewarm church. Ephesians 5:27 expresses the hope "that the church might be presented before him in splendor, without spot or wrinkle or any such thing, that she might be holy and without blemish," but it is evident that this is yet a hope rather than a full actuality.

The New Testament churches were not wholly united. Paul and Barnabas had a sharp contention and went in different directions; the Corinthian church contained four factions; the Jewish church and the Gentile church found it difficult to agree, and the Jerusalem conference was occasioned by the disagreements.

The churches of the New Testament varied from one another in many things. There was variety in the expression of doctrine, as one realizes from reading Paul, John, and Hebrews, for example. There was diversity in organization and practice. I Corinthians 12:28 mentions apostles, prophets, teachers, workers of miracles, healers, helpers, administrators, speakers in various kinds of tongues; the pastoral epistles speak of bishops, deacons, and elders. The Jerusalem church practiced community of property; in other churches there is no sign of it.

But though we cannot expect to find a complete and perfect blueprint in the New Testament for the life of the church today, we cannot fail to find in it upon careful study many things which provide indispensable guidance and inspiration for the church today as it seeks to move forward.

For one thing, although the New Testament church was not perfect it was in closest proximity to Jesus Christ. Here we stand closest to the event with which Christianity was founded, the life, death, and resurrection of Jesus Christ. Some of the members of the New Testament church had heard Jesus teach, some had stood in the shadow of his cross, some had experienced his resurrection. Some of the authors of New Testament documents had been eyewitnesses of some of the happenings, others had gathered materials from those who were eyewitnesses from the beginning. Since Christianity is so profoundly a historical religion, we shall always have to go back to the New Testament church and to the New Testament records which it produced, in order to learn as much as we can about Jesus Christ in whom God's chief revelation was given.

Again, although divisions and difficulties existed then as now, the New Testament church had a great ideal of unity. The Gospels which tell how the disciples disputed at the Last Supper as to "which of them was to be regarded as the greatest," state also that on the same occasion Jesus prayed for all his followers "that they may all be one . . . so that the world may believe"; and the Pauline letters which record the disagreements at Corinth and elsewhere, contain too the appeal "that all of you agree that there be no dissensions among you, but that you be united," and the affirmation that "there is one body and one Spirit . . . one Lord, one faith, one baptism, one God and Father of us all."[2] Thus what Charles Clayton Morrison calls its "overarching ecumenical character"[3] is the most outstanding feature of the New Testament church, and the restoration of the New Testament church can consist in nothing less than the recovery of its ecumenical ideal and the pressing on toward its goal of Christian unity.

Furthermore, although there was much variety in the details of the life of the New Testament church, there was also agreement upon many fundamentals. In the realm of doctrine there were different ideas about the end of the world, for example, but there was unanimity of belief in God and in Jesus Christ. With the substance and significance of this Christian faith in God and in Christ we were concerned in the two preceding sections of this book. In the realm of practice different things were done. Not every practice was universal. At Jerusalem the disciples "had all things in common,"[4] but community of property is not mentioned in connection with the Pauline churches. Not everything that was done went back to Jesus. The phenomenon of speaking with tongues was known both at Jerusalem and in the Pauline churches, but no one claimed Jesus had spoken with tongues or had in any way originated the practice. Incidentally, the fact that the Gospels say nothing of such speaking with tongues is an item of evidence on the side of believing that the Gospels basically provide an objective account of the life of Jesus rather than chiefly a reflection of the conditions in the later church.

Not everything that was done in the New Testament church was expected by its own wise leaders to be permanent. In spite of the fact that he himself spoke with tongues, Paul said, "tongues will cease."[5] But of other things in the practice of the New Testament church it can be said that they were evidently universal, being found in the Jerusalem church, in the Hellenistic churches, and in the churches established by Paul; that they definitely went back to Jesus, being based upon what he himself had done or said; and that they were, as far as the references to them suggest, expected to be continuing features of the church's life. Such features of New Testament church practice presumably, therefore, have special importance for the church today. Two items which appear to have been universal among the early Christians, to have originated with Jesus himself, and to have been looked upon as permanent elements in church practice, were baptism and the Lord's Supper. To the study of these the next two chapters will be devoted. Finally, in the area of experience, there was undoubtedly variety too. But there was agreement that essentially Christian experience had to do with Christ. It is what Charles Clayton Morrison calls this "transcendent loyalty" to Christ,[6] which is being rediscovered in our time and which is again, beyond all diverseness and divisiveness, drawing the denominations together.

CHAPTER TWENTY-ONE

The Meaning of Baptism

Baptism has been a practice of most of the churches throughout the centuries, but there are many differences of opinion about it. There is difference in the importance attached to baptism. One church regards baptism as of such very great importance that it takes its own name from the practice. Another believes that outward baptism is entirely unimportant, and does not practice an outward baptism at all. Between these two extremes, there are various intermediate positions. There is difference of opinion as to how baptism is to be performed. In some churches, baptism is conducted by sprinkling some water on a person; in some churches, by pouring a somewhat more liberal quantity of water upon a person; in some churches, by dipping the person underneath the surface of the water and out again; and in some churches, by dipping the person underneath the water and out again three times in succession.

There is difference of judgment as to who it is that should be baptized. Some churches teach that infants should be baptized as soon as it is practically possible, and that there may even be grave danger if this is not done immediately. Others teach that baptism is something which should be performed only for those who are adult, or at least grown up enough to think for themselves and to choose the act on their own volition. There is also difference of interpretation as to what baptism means. Two large churches in the world perform the ceremony in virtually identical outward fashion. From the manner in which the rite is conducted it is doubtful if a spectator could tell in which church he was. Yet a difference of opinion in the interpretation of the significance of what is done, has been a chief factor in keeping the two churches apart for many years. That the point at issue is so subtle that many members and even ministers in both groups would be hard put to explain it clearly, does not keep it from being a major stumbling block on the road to Christian union.

In addition to the inherent difficulties attaching to the several problems just listed, there is the fact that we now have a heritage of dispute over the matter. It is related that Lloyd George was once driving through North Wales with a friend when they fell to discussing denominational differences. "The church I belong to," said Lloyd George, "is torn with a fierce dispute. One section says that baptism is *in* the name of the Father, and the other that it is *into* the name of the Father. I belong to one of these parties. I feel most strongly about it. I would die for it in fact—but I forget which it is!" So it is that a heritage of dispute may persist long after the relevance of the dispute is in the past.

In discussing a matter concerning which the churches

honestly differ, it is evident that we must maintain a sincere respect for the conscientious belief of other persons. Yet it is also necessary to make a thorough study of the subject for ourselves, and desirable that we state humbly but plainly the conclusions to which we come. And as we do it we must also maintain the hope for larger unity. To respect one another fully, and converse with one another honestly, are necessary aspects of participation in the ecumenical movement. In what follows we will endeavor to gain an understanding of baptism that will be scriptural, sensible, and spiritual.

Scriptural

In view of the basic belief of the reformed churches that the life of the church can be renewed, guided, and inspired by going back to the Bible, we shall wish to study what is said about baptism in the Scriptures. In answer to the question as to whether baptism is important, we find that it plays a large role in the New Testament. The practice was found in Jewish, Hellenistic, and Pauline churches alike; it was commended by the act of Jesus himself in being baptized at the beginning of his ministry; and from the references to it in the epistles it was evidently assumed that it would be a continuing feature of church procedure. The words "baptism," "baptize," and "baptist" occur more than one hundred times in the New Testament text.

How was baptism performed? In the Greek New Testament the word meaning to baptize is readily recognizable by persons speaking almost any modern European language, for it is *baptizein* which has passed through Latin *baptizare* into French *baptiser,* Spanish *bautizar,* Italian *battezzare,* and English *baptize.* Only German translates with a word from a different root, *taufen,* and as we shall at once see this still ties in with the basic meaning of the Greek word for it comes from *Tiefe* meaning "deep" or "depth." When the Greek word *baptizein* is looked up in any Greek lexicon it is found that its primary meaning is to dip, immerse, or sink. The word occurs in the works of more than thirty Greek authors, from Pindar in the sixth century B.C. to Eustathius in the eleventh century A.D. with the same basic meaning. These writers were of course discussing many things other than baptism in the Christian church. One was speaking about a ship which sank, and he said that it was "baptized" in the ocean when it went under. Another was talking about the process of tempering metal, and he said that when the mass of iron was drawn red hot from the furnace it was "baptized" in water. Thus *baptizein* was simply the ordinary word used by those who spoke Greek when they wished to convey the idea of dipping or immersing.

Jesus himself probably spoke Aramaic in his ordinary conversation and teaching, since that was the most common language of the people of Palestine at that time. In Aramaic the word corresponding to Greek *baptizein,* is *tebal,* which likewise means to dip or immerse. Discussing these words with reference to the baptism of Jesus by John, Carl H. Kraeling writes: "Immersion is thus the natural implication of the terminology and must be regarded as the normal procedure in the original performance of the rite."[1]

Not only the word which describes the act, but also

the circumstances in which baptism was performed, as examples are narrated in the New Testament, show that for John the Baptist, Jesus, and the early Christians, baptism consisted in immersion in water. It was evidently because the act was of this sort that John the Baptist chose the Jordan River as the place to conduct the rite in which Jesus and so many others participated. Later he baptized "at Aenon near Salim, because there was much water there."[2] In immediate connection with this last reference, is found the statement about the baptisms conducted by Jesus and his disciples, so it may be presumed that they were of the same sort. Again, in the records of the apostolic church we have such an account as that of the conversion of the Ethiopian eunuch by Philip: "And as they went along the road they came to some water, and the eunuch said, 'See, here is water! What is to prevent my being baptized?' . . . And they both went down into the water, Philip and the eunuch, and he baptized him."[3]

A doubt may be expressed by some concerning the reported baptism of about three thousand persons at Jerusalem on the day of Pentecost, to the effect that in a city where until recent times water was very scarce these baptisms could hardly have been performed in the manner indicated above. But in actuality there were available such places as the well-known Pool of Siloam, fed by the waters of the spring of Gihon, and the Pool of Bethesda down into which, as John 5:7 tells us, invalids went in the hope of healing. The latter place was probably in the vicinity of the present Church of St. Anne north of the Temple area in Jerusalem. There archeologists have traced the outlines of a large double pool once surrounded by fine balustrades and galleries. The area occupied was over 5,000 square yards in extent, and the situation was such as to facilitate the collection of rain water, by which the pools were supplied through a system of conduits. The excavators themselves surmise the use of the Pool of Bethesda for Christian baptism in early times.[4]

It also seems probable that even as Christian baptism had a connection with the foregoing practice of baptism by John the Baptist, so too John's baptism had some relationship to the practice of baptism in the receiving of proselytes into the Jewish faith. Proselyte baptism is described in the Jewish Talmud, where we are told that the candidate stood in water and immersed himself in the presence of two appointed witnesses. This item of evidence, therefore, if it does have any connection with the rise of Christian baptism, is in agreement with the conclusion that the way in which the latter rite was performed was by immersion.

Who was baptized? In answer to this question it may be said that every time in the New Testament when we are told about the baptism of an identifiable individual, it is someone who is clearly old enough to know what he is doing. It is true that in such cases as Acts 16:15 where Lydia is said to have been baptized "with her household," and Acts 16:33 where the Philippian jailer is reported to have been baptized "with all his family," we cannot identify all the individuals involved and may wish to suppose that the "household" of the one person or the "family" of the other included infants. But that infants were actually baptized on these or other occasions can only be a supposition, and as a matter of fact is extremely unlikely inasmuch as the Christian message seems regularly to have been presented as a call to decision, to which only persons capable of understanding could be expected to respond.

And how is baptism to be interpreted? In the New Testament it is set forth as the way into the Christian life. "Brethren, what shall we do?" asked those who heard Peter speak on the day of Pentecost, and he replied: "Repent, and be baptized every one of you in the name of Jesus Christ for the forgiveness of your sins; and you shall receive the gift of the Holy Spirit."[5] "Men, what must I do to be saved?" inquired the jailer at Philippi, and after he heard the reply of the apostles that he must believe in the Lord Jesus, "he was baptized at once, with all his family."[6]

In the pages of the New Testament, therefore, we find what seem to be quite clear answers to the questions we have asked about baptism. This fundamental understanding is also confirmed by much in later church history, and in particular baptism as immersion is long found as the standard practice. Tertullian, writing *On Baptism* in about A.D. 200, tells how not only John baptized in the Jordan, but also Peter in the Tiber. The baptistery of the Church of St. Menas, built in the Egyptian desert in about A.D. 400 and excavated by modern archeologists, was obviously intended for immersion, being a deep marble tank, entered by steps from either side. Thomas Aquinas, authoritative spokesman for the Roman Catholic church, said in the thirteenth century, "The common practice is immersion." In the Eastern Orthodox church, immersion has continued to be the standard procedure until today.

Nevertheless, not long after New Testament times, modifications of practice began to be made for convenience and other reasons. In the second century, the writing known as *The Teaching of the Twelve Apostles* referred to immersion in running water as the usual method but allowed for other procedures in case of necessity:

> And concerning baptism, thus baptize ye: Having first said all these things, baptize into the name of the Father, and of the Son, and of the Holy Spirit, in living water. But if thou have not living water, baptize into other water; and if thou have not either, pour out water thrice upon the head into the name of Father and Son and Holy Spirit.

Likewise, as to the persons who are to be baptized, there is a probable reference to the baptism of infants in Irenaeus, who wrote about A.D. 180, and by the fifth century infant rather than adult baptism was becoming somewhat general practice.

Sensible

Does baptism as we find it in the scriptural records make sense as we think about it today? Yes, as presented in the New Testament and as we have endeavored to describe it above, baptism is reasonable. It is a complete baptism and thus is fitting as a mark of entry into the Christian life, which means a complete commitment. The Christian life involves the head, the hands, the feet, and the whole self, and thus it is fitting that the ceremony of entrance into that life likewise involve the whole person. It is significant that outstanding leaders of the two great streams of the Protestant Reformation, the Lutheran church and the Reformed church, have commented affirmatively on this very point. Martin Luther used the word "complete" with regard to baptism. In his work *On the Babylonish Captivity of the Church,* the founder of the Protestant Reformation wrote:

> In Greek to baptize signifies to dip, and baptism is a dipping. . . . For this reason I could wish that the baptized should be totally immersed, according to the meaning of the word and the signification of the mystery; not that I think it necessary to do so, but that it would be well that so complete and perfect a thing as baptism should have its sign also in completeness and perfection, even as it was doubtless instituted by Christ.

It will of course be noted that in this otherwise consistent statement about practicing a complete baptism, Luther inserted almost parenthetically the qualification: "not that I think it necessary to do so." As we know, his followers generally emphasized the qualification, and did not feel it necessary to conduct baptism by immersion. Nevertheless it is clear that Luther's real feeling about the matter was that baptism ought to be something as complete as a Christian's complete commitment to the Christian way of life.

The same opinion is advanced by Karl Barth, probably the most prominent theologian of the other great stream of the Protestant heritage, that of the Reformed church. Barth has written a small book entitled *Die kirchliche Lehre von der Taufe,* the third edition of which was published in 1947. In it he says:

> One can scarcely deny that the baptism which was conducted even in the West as immersion until deep in the Middle Ages

was much more expressive as a sign of what baptism has to represent, than the infusion which then became customary, especially after this was rendered innocuous by being changed in practice from an actual pouring to a sprinkling and finally to a simple moistening with as little water as possible. Who would yet think from this that Paul had seen the prototype of baptism in such a critical experience as the passage of the Israelites through the Red Sea (I Corinthians 10:1 f.)? One can really agree with Luther in the opinion that it would be fine if such a complete and significant thing were also given its significant and complete sign: *sicut et institutum est sine dubio a Christo* [as it was doubtless instituted by Christ].[7]

Again, others in the same church do not feel it necessary to follow what is here suggested; nevertheless the logic seems inescapable: baptism is most meaningful when it is a complete baptism.

Another mark of the New Testament baptism which commends it as reasonable may be indicated by calling it responsible baptism. This is baptism of a person who is old enough to be responsible for what he is doing, who is doing it as a responsible act, and with the intention on his own part of living up to the meaning of the act. As Luther introduced the word "complete" in his discussion of baptism and was followed by Barth, so Barth also employs this word "responsible." He writes:

Baptism is in the New Testament the indispensable answer to an unavoidable question made by the man who comes to faith. . . . In baptism a restoration is called for. What is demanded is very simple: in place of the present infant baptism a responsible baptism on the part of the person being baptized. He must, if things are to be done right, become once again not a passive object of baptism but the free partner of Jesus Christ, who decides for himself, confesses for himself, and testifies for himself to his own willingness and readiness.[8]

Unless baptism is thus the responsible act of a responsible person, it may not always be taken seriously. Professor William Robinson, formerly of Overdale College, Birmingham, England, has cited these figures: In England about 67 out of 100 children born are baptized in the Church of England. Not more than 26 of these are later confirmed in the church, and only 9 become faithful members.[9] The difference between the 67 who were baptized as infants and the 9 who became faithful members of the church obviously represents the large group for whom baptism was an irresponsible thing. They did not originally choose it by their own volition, and they now have no intention of living up to what was done without their choice.

Yet another mark of baptism as we have seen it in the New Testament is that it is hard. It was doubtless the desire to have an easier and more convenient way of performing the rite that led to some of the modifications in its practice. A German writer today, discussing this problem and defending an entirely different view of baptism, commends other modes because of "ease of administration, healthfulness, and propriety." But are such considerations as these the ones chiefly to have in mind in the beginning of the Christian life? Is not the Christian life itself something which is difficult rather than easy, and something in which the criterion is higher than conformity to the approved practices of the world? If so, is it not reasonable and well that the ceremony of beginning is itself distinctive and even difficult?

Spiritual

We have sought for a scriptural and reasonable understanding of baptism, but most important of all, of course, is an understanding of its spiritual meaning. As found in the New Testament and as set forth above, baptism is an outward ceremony, but an outward ceremony is meaningless unless it corresponds to an inward reality. To what inward reality, then, does baptism correspond? What spiritual meaning does it have as it is performed? What does it bring to the one who is baptized? At least the following is suggested by the New Testament: Baptism brings an assurance of sonship: it was when Jesus was being baptized that the heavenly voice spoke to him as Son. Baptism brings an assurance of discipleship: the one being baptized is following in an act of Jesus himself. Baptism brings an assurance of salvation: to Titus, working among the proverbially corrupt Cretans, it was written, "He saved us . . . by the washing of regeneration."[10] Baptism brings us assurance of new life and the resurrection: "We are buried therefore with him by baptism into death, so that as Christ was raised from the dead by the glory of the Father, we too might walk in newness of life."[11] As Karl Barth wrote:

> In its essential nature Christian baptism is the picture of the renewing of man through his participation by the power of the Holy Spirit in the death and resurrection of Jesus Christ and therewith it is the picture of man's being brought into association with him, with the covenant of grace made and realized in him, and with the fellowship of his church. . . . What baptism pictures . . . is an eminently critical experience: the participa-

tion of the man who is being baptized in the death and resurrection of Jesus Christ, the fact that then and there in the year 30 before the gate of Jerusalem on the cross of Golgotha not only Jesus Christ but also this man with him died eternally, and that in the garden of Joseph of Arimathea not only Jesus Christ but also this man with him is eternally raised from the dead.[12]

Not less profound and tremendous than that is the spiritual meaning of baptism. Since it is the spiritual meaning of baptism which is of paramount importance, and since most Christians are no doubt in substantial agreement about it, our opinions concerning lesser matters such as the method by which baptism is to be performed must always be held with such charity and considerateness of the differing views of others that we shall not put an obstruction in the way of the growth of Christian co-operation by the expression of our best understanding, but rather contribute in humility what we can to the richness of the emerging structure of the ecumenical church for which we hope.[13]

CHAPTER TWENTY-TWO

The Significance of the Lord's Supper

A second observance which seems to have been universal in the New Testament churches, which originated in what Jesus himself did, which was spoken of by early church leaders as if it were a permanent part of church life, and which has in fact been continued in almost all the churches ever since, is that which is variously known as breaking bread, Communion, the Eucharist, or the Lord's Supper.[1] As baptism was the service of entrance into the church, so this was the service of fellowship within the church. It was a continuation of the table fellowship of Jesus and his disciples, since during his ministry they must have often eaten together, and in particular it was a commemoration of the very last meal they ate together on the eve of his death.

The Last Supper

What happened at the time of the last supper of Jesus and his disciples? At that time the Jews observed the Passover. Spring came, and they watched the western sky at evening until the thin crescent of the new moon appeared. At that point they reckoned the beginning of a new month and the beginning of a new year. The month, the first of the new year, was called Nisan. Since they considered that the new day began at nightfall, rather than at midnight as we do, the first day of the new month began the same evening that the new moon was first seen. Then they counted fifteen days and on the fifteenth of Nisan, when the moon was in full splendor, they observed the Passover.

The law governing this observance can still be read in the twelfth chapter of Exodus. It prescribes that on the tenth day of Nisan each household should pick out a lamb or a kid and keep it carefully. On the fourteenth day of the month the animal was to be slain "between the two evenings,"[2] a time which Josephus explains was from the ninth to the eleventh hour, that is from three to five o'clock in the afternoon.[3] After that the sacrificial animal was put on to roast, and all waited for the night. This day when the lamb was slain was known as the Preparation for the Passover, or the eve of Passover. In the year A.D. 30 the fourteenth day of Nisan corresponded to April 7 in our calendar. When night came, the new day, the fifteenth of Nisan, began and the Passover meal was held. Along with the roast meat the meal consisted of unleavened bread and bitter herbs. All was eaten in haste and under strict command that nothing of the sacrificial animal should be left until morning. So they remembered how their fathers ate in haste on the night of their departure from Egypt, and how mightily God acted to deliver them from the land of bondage. It was the birthday observance of their national life. Thus the Jewish people celebrated their Passover.

It was at this time of year that Jesus ate his last meal with his disciples. It may have been that this meal was the Passover feast. Some of the Gospels indicate that it was,[4] but even they contain points which make one wonder if it could actually have been that meal. They say nothing, for example, about any roast lamb which would certainly have been a part of a Passover meal. What is more, they tell how after the supper Jesus went out to Gethsemane and was arrested there, and how during the night he was brought before the Sanhedrin and tried, then the next morning turned over to Pilate by whom he was condemned to death and executed. Now it is difficult to understand how the Jewish Sanhedrin, that august body of priests, elders, and scribes, could have had such a meeting at the very time when, by the Law, faithful Jews were bound to be engaged in the observance of the Passover, the most sacred festival of the entire religious year. As a matter of fact it is reported that when they began to conspire against Jesus to accomplish his death, they said, "Not during the feast, lest there be a tumult of the people."[5]

The first three Gospels thus describe the Last Supper as a Passover meal but at the same time contain points which make one wonder how it could have been that meal itself; the Fourth Gospel lets us understand that the Last Supper actually took place one night before the Passover meal. John 19:14 states that it was the day of Preparation for the Passover when Jesus was condemned by Pilate; thus he died on the cross of Golgotha on the same day that the Passover lambs were slain. As Paul wrote in I Corinthians 5:7, "Christ, our paschal lamb, has been sacrificed." The Jewish Talmud also gives this same date for the crucifixion, when it says that Jesus was put to death "on the eve of Passover." According to these statements we would date the death of Jesus on the fourteenth day of Nisan, April 7 in the year A.D. 30, and therefore the Last Supper would have taken place one day earlier than that and one day earlier than the Passover feast.

The historical problem thus presented may be insoluble at the present time; in the future new evidence may appear from some source now unknown which will enable us to see a solution to the difficulty. But there is one short enigmatical passage in the Gospels which may possibly hold the clue even now. This is Luke 22:15-16 where at the Last Supper Jesus says to the disciples, "I have earnestly desired to eat this passover with you before I suffer; for I tell you I shall not eat it until it is fulfilled in the kingdom of God." The difficulty of the passage is shown by the fact that a number of manuscripts changed the last part to read: "for I tell you I shall never eat it again until it is fulfilled in the kingdom of God." This reading provides no difficulty. The Last Supper was the Passover; at it Jesus spoke of how much he had desired to eat the Passover with the disciples; anticipating his death he predicted that he would not eat the Passover *again* until in the kingdom of God. But the overwhelming majority of the most ancient manuscripts give the passage in the form in which we quoted it first, which is that found in the Revised Standard Version as printed in 1953. Not only do the best manuscripts support this reading, it is also harder to understand and thus it is more probable that the harder reading was changed in some manuscripts into a more intelligible form, than that the easier reading existed first of all and was changed into the harder. Taking the verse then in what seems more probably its original form, Jesus said, in effect, that he had deeply wished to live to eat the Passover meal with his disciples that spring, but that since, as he now saw, he would die before the Passover came he would not be able to eat it until in the kingdom of God. Therefore it must be that the meal they were then eating together, the last they were so to enjoy, was one held before the Passover, perhaps even an anticipatory Passover meal, not however on Passover night but the night before.[6]

The Lord's Supper

Next we have to speak of what Jesus made of that last meal. If we continue to follow the Gospel according to Luke and the best manuscripts, we find that Jesus began the meal by taking a cup, giving thanks, and giving it to the disciples to divide among themselves, saying that from then on he would not drink of the fruit of the vine until the kingdom of God came. This could have been the *kiddush* as the Jewish people call it, the ceremony to hallow a special occasion when the rabbi or leader blesses a cup, sips from it, and passes it to the others participating. Then Jesus took bread, gave thanks, broke it, and gave it to the disciples. This was a usual way for the head of a group to inaugurate a common meal. Doubtless Jesus had done it many times before as he and the disciples ate together. But this time he spoke additional words of the most solemn import. He said, "This is my body." Then they continued with the meal, and only "after supper" did he give them another cup. At that time he said, "This cup which is poured out for you is the new covenant in my blood." It is true that at this point some of the ancient manuscripts leave out this last part about the cup, and they are manuscripts which are usually quite dependable in their very omissions. On the other hand, at this place their scribes may have thought that it was too much to have the two cups, and so may have made the omission deliberately. At any rate, if the meal did begin with a cup we can explain it as the *kiddush*; and we have Matthew, Mark, and Paul as well as Luke to tell us about the bread which Jesus said was his body and the cup which he said was his blood of the covenant.

Since Jesus was at the table with them when he said that the bread was his body and the cup his blood, the disciples must have understood plainly that he meant that the bread and the cup were symbols of his body and blood. He was telling them that even as the bread was broken in his hands so his body was soon going to be broken by his enemies, and even as the cup was poured out so his blood was going to be shed. They could not miss the meaning of that. And when he referred to the covenant in connection with his blood, they must have understood that well too. At the Passover season everybody recalled the exodus from Egypt. It was then that the children of Israel went to Mount Sinai and made their covenant with their God. To ratify that covenant animals were sacrificed and their blood sprinkled on the altar. Now Jesus was telling them that he was about to shed his blood to ratify a new covenant between God and man.

And what did the disciples do? They kept on, afterward, eating together. They doubtless did not have roast lamb on their tables very often; sometimes they had fish and always they must have had bread and something to drink. So always when they broke the loaf and passed the cup they remembered how they had formerly eaten together with their Master, and in particular they remembered what he had said about the bread and the cup at the very last supper of all. According to Luke 22:19 and I Corinthians 11:24-25 he had told them at that time to do this in remembrance of him. Even without such a command they could scarcely have failed to do so.

At first they broke bread together every day, as Acts 2:46 relates. Later, as Acts 20:7 states, they did it "on the first day of the week," that is on Sunday, the anniversary day of the resurrection of Jesus, and this became the regular custom. To the observance the name the Lord's Supper was given, or one of the other designations cited at the beginning of this chapter. As long as it continued to be a complete meal it was also sometimes called the *Agape* or Love Feast, as in Jude 12. But as Jude shows and as we learn already from Paul's correspondence with Corinth, abuses crept into the common meals. "In eating," as Paul described it at Corinth, "each one goes ahead with his own meal, and one is hungry and another is drunk." "What!" he went on, "do you not have houses to eat and drink in?"[7] As this expostulation suggested, the complete meal was gradually dropped from the church service, and in it only symbolic portions of food and drink were consumed.

As Justin Martyr described the church service of about A.D. 150 it went like this:

> On the day called the Day of the Sun there is a gathering in one place of us all who live in cities or in the country, and the memoirs of the apostles or the writings of the prophets are read as long as time allows. Then, when the reader has ceased, the president gives by word of mouth his admonition and exhortation to imitate these excellent things. Afterward we all rise at once and offer prayers. . . . Thereupon to the president of the brethren bread and a cup of water and wine are brought, and he takes it and offers up praise and glory to the Father of the universe through the name of the Son and the Holy Spirit, and gives thanks at length that we have been accounted worthy of these things from him; and when he has ended the prayers and thanksgiving the whole people present assent, saying "Amen." . . . Then after the president has given thanks and all the people have assented, those who are called by us deacons give to each one of those present to partake of the bread and of the wine and water for which thanks have been given, and for those not present they take away a portion.[8]

The Living Supper

Thus the last supper of Jesus and the disciples became the Lord's Supper and is until today the living supper of the church. It signifies remembrance of Jesus. Tangible elements provide for an acted parable in which his death is recalled. To the church it also means experience of Christ. To the disciples who journeyed to Emmaus, the risen Christ was made known "in the breaking of the bread."[9] In at least one branch of the church the doctrine was developed that in the eucharistic service the bread and the wine are actually transformed into the body and blood of Christ and so he is present in that very literal way; to many other branches of the church it seems rather that his presence is a spiritual fact. But the Lord's Supper signifies not only remembrance and experience but also expectation. It constitutes a forward look to the ultimate victory of Jesus Christ. "As often as you eat this bread and drink the cup, you proclaim the Lord's death until he comes."[10] So it points us to the hope of the church.

> Bread of the world in mercy broken,
> Wine of the soul in mercy shed,
> By whom the words of life were spoken,
> And in whose death our sins are dead;
>
> Look on the heart by sorrow broken,
> Look on the tears by sinners shed;
> And be Thy feast to us the token
> That by Thy grace our souls are fed.

CHAPTER TWENTY-THREE

The Hope of the Church

It is well that the church is set in the midst of the world as the custodian of a significant hope, because the present situation is one in which that is needed.

The Present Situation

There is much lack of hope at the present time. The description of the Gentiles in Ephesians 2:12 as "having no hope" would characterize much of our secular world. This period of one hundred years was optimistically expected to be the "century of progress," but it is scarcely more than half gone and anticipation of possible disaster quite overshadows confidence in achievement. Hopelessness, which is far more characteristic of our age than hope, is often compounded of a sense of failure, frustration, and fear. The failures of the past reach after us in the present. Many situations both in individual lives and in national and international affairs exhibit that aspect of tragedy which consists in the fact that so many wrong choices have been made in the past that no choice in the present can be without disastrous effects. Frustration exists where the circumstances of life seem more than we can handle. It was exhibited in personal life by the California housewife who burned down the house which she despaired of ever being able to keep tidy, and by the man who told his minister how much he hated liquor but how he had to use it because it was the only thing he knew which could get him away from himself. Fear is only too evident throughout the entire world, as the ominous shadow of atomic destruction haunts the minds of men who have set loose this tremendous power. The ultimate expression of this hopelessness is in the complete despair of the atheistic philosophy known as existentialism.

There are also, however, many false or insufficient hopes abroad in the world. The prophecy of Mark 13:22 that "false Christs . . . will arise," has been abundantly verified. Some of these false prophets have been discredited, others still beguile the unsuspecting. Evolutionism, which seemed in the past century to guarantee perpetual and inevitable progress, is largely discredited. Scientism, which made a fetish of genuine science and looked to it for the solution of all man's problems, has been disavowed by many of the leaders of science themselves who stress that something more than the production of more machines is needed for man's salvation. Humanism, which supposes man's destiny to lie wholly in his own hands and his salvation to be possible wholly from his own resources, has many followers; yet the ultimate crises of life find almost every person crying out for help from a higher source. Racism, which was to be the foundation of an empire that would endure for a thousand years, was in that case revealed for the false teaching that it is, yet in other forms lurks elsewhere, leading those of a certain color of skin to suppose a superiority and trust in a supremacy that are the gravest of illusions. Socialism was expected by some to be the solution to human ills, but not long ago the most trusted leader of the movement in the United States of America said: "The working class is not the Messiah which some of us thought"; neither is socialism "a panacea against war."[1] Nationalism now exercises a potent influence and rouses great expectations in most of the countries of Asia and other relatively undeveloped parts of the earth, yet certainly carries with it many dangers, as the modern history of Europe amply illustrates. Communism bases its appeal upon what it promises for the welfare of the common man, yet when once in control proceeds rapidly to the enslavement of everybody. To hope in something and find it a false hope is almost more bitter than not to hope at all, yet that is exactly the experience of many.

But again it must be noted that there is misinterpreted hope as well as false hope and hopelessness. It is even possible that the church has held a hope before men which it has interpreted wrongly, and has therefore not led them well. When the church has interpreted the gospel as meaning that the literal end of the world would take place very soon, at a date which could be determined by manipulation of biblical prophecy and was actually announced for a precise year, and has advised its members in view of the imminent end to lay down their tasks and wait for God's immediately forthcoming action, it has set forth a teaching quite at variance with the parables of Jesus in which he told of stewards faithfully continuing the exercise of their responsibilities during the absence of their master, and at variance with the explicit command: "Take heed, watch; for you do not know when the time will come."[2] Yet just because the church has sometimes misinterpreted the hope with which it is entrusted, we must proceed with humility and care to set forth as well as we can the true hope which we are given.

The True Hope

According to the New Testament, the hope of the church is twofold. It is a hope for the kingdom of God and for the coming of Christ. The hope for the kingdom is expressed in the prayer Jesus taught his disciples, which has been used in the church throughout the whole world ever since. After the salutation to God as the Father in heaven, and the expression of reverence for his name, the first entreaty of the prayer is: "Thy kingdom come."[3]

What is the kingdom? The answer is given by the words of the prayer which follow immediately: "Thy will be done." The kingdom of God is the reign of God. When the kingdom comes, the will of God will be done. Since that will is opposed to all evil and turned to all good, nothing higher than this can be desired. When will the kingdom come? In one way it has already come. When Jesus was on earth he said to men, "The kingdom of God is in the midst of you."[4] The kingdom is also coming. In not a few of the parables of Jesus concerning the kingdom, the central idea is that of growth. The kingdom will come in the future. It is not here yet in its fullness when evil is still at work and destroying the innocent. But God will not be defeated, and at last his kingdom will come. Where will the kingdom be? Again the Lord's prayer gives an answer: "On earth as it is in heaven." The hope of the church is for a kingdom of God upon earth. This is also expressed in the book of Revelation in the conception of the millennium.[5] One need not insist upon taking the thousand years literally, indeed in view of the symbolic character of the language throughout the book of Revelation it is doubtful if the author meant it to be taken that way, but one can hardly mistake the fact that a hope is being set forth here for a time in which Christ will truly hold sway in the lives of men upon earth. Yet the hope of the church is not exhausted with an earthly expectation. After the millennium, the seer of the Revelation saw that "earth and sky fled away," and "a new heaven and a new earth" came into being.[6] This certainly implies a new world which lies beyond all earthly history. It is there that God will dwell with men, and that "he will wipe away every tear from their eyes, and death shall be no more, neither shall there be mourning nor crying nor pain any more, for the former things have passed away."[7] And for whom is this kingdom intended? According to Colossians 1:20 it was the purpose of God in Christ "to reconcile to himself all things," and according to II Peter 3:9 he is "not wishing that any should perish, but that all should reach repentance."

The other aspect of the twofold hope of the church is the hope for the coming of Christ. There is another prayer which the early church used as well as the Lord's prayer. The one prayer was taught by Jesus himself; this one must have originated in the earliest Palestinian church because it is still preserved in Aramaic, the common language of Palestine at that time. The fact that it was handed down in the original Aramaic shows how much it meant as the traditional supplication of the church and, as a matter of fact, it was still being used in Aramaic in the second century as may be seen in *The Teaching of the Twelve Apostles* where it occurs as a part of the prayers to be used at the Eucharist. In the New Testament it is quoted in Aramaic in I Corinthians 16:22. Here Paul had taken the pen in his own hand to add his closing words in the letter in his own handwriting. Although he wrote in Greek he did not translate the prayer, but put it down in Aramaic. It was very short: *Marana tha.* It meant, "Our Lord, come!"

What is the coming of Christ? It is the same as the coming of the kingdom. He is the King of that kingdom. It was his coming which marked the coming of the kingdom. He said: "If it is by the finger of God that I cast out demons, then the kingdom of God has come upon you"; "The queen of the South will arise at the judgment with the men of this generation and condemn them; for she came from the ends of the earth to hear the wisdom of Solomon, and behold, something greater than Solomon is here."[8] Even so, when God's kingdom comes in the future, the King, once rejected, will be vindicated. When will the coming of Christ be? It is an oversimplification to answer this question by referring only to the "second coming." That is a phrase which occurs first in the writings of Justin Martyr and is not in the New Testament. The New Testament refers to many "comings" of

Christ. He came already in his historical ministry. He came back in his resurrection. He is coming in the hearts of those who will accept him now.

> No ear may hear His coming,
> But in this world of sin,
> Where meek souls will receive Him still,
> The dear Christ enters in.

He comes at the death of his followers to receive them to himself. He will come in the reign of righteousness upon earth, and he will be the head of his people in the kingdom which is beyond history.

After an analysis of the various passages in the Gospels which have to do with the coming of Christ, C. H. Dodd writes:

> So we seem to be left with several groups of sayings which on the face of them point in different directions. Sometimes, it seems, they associate the coming of the Son of Man in glory, the kingdom of God, and the Last Judgment, with the historical ministry of Jesus Christ; sometimes they associate it with historical crises yet to come; and sometimes with that which lies beyond all history, in another world than this.
>
> I put it to you that He meant all these, and all at once. . . . Let me remind you that poets very often use language with just such a double meaning; one meaning on the surface, another beneath the surface. . . . That is the way poets see life; not all on one level, but depth below depth. . . . The human mind of Jesus Christ was a poet's mind. That stands out on every page of the Gospels. Where others saw only incidents in the career of a rustic prophet who came to a sad end, He saw the great Day of the Lord; not only saw it, but acted it out. He saw that Day come, in the brief spell when He worked and suffered in Palestine. He saw it extended into history yet to be. He saw it extended into the world beyond history, where alone the kingdom of God can be perfectly revealed. And yet it was *there*, really and actually. The Day had come.[9]

This, then, is the hope of the church and the true hope of the world, the hope for the coming of the kingdom of God and the hope for the coming of Christ.

The Effect of Hope

It is the effect of hope to give life. "By his great mercy we have been born anew to a living hope through the resurrection of Jesus Christ from the dead."[10] We commonly say that while there is life there is hope. The converse is true: while there is hope there is life. "Where there is no hope," wrote Samuel Johnson, "there can be no endeavor." Where there is hope, there cannot but be endeavor. Hope makes alive. It is because the church has hope that the church lives. The hope is grounded in faith and expressed in love. Together these three verities, hope, faith, and love, abide. If he believes his faith with his emotions as well as with his intellect, the Christian can never be entirely discouraged. Even though he is disappointed and defeated he tries again, for he believes in a power greater than his own and a purpose which goes beyond his own understanding. Though he is perplexed he is not driven to despair, and though he is struck down he is not destroyed. The confidence which Christians have, comes from "knowing that he who raised the Lord Jesus will raise us also with Jesus and bring us with you into his presence."[11]

Notes

INTRODUCTION

Chapter 2. Mystery in Religion

1 I Corinthians 13:12.

2 Mark 4:11; I Corinthians 2:7, King James Version.

3 *The Scofield Reference Bible* (New York: Oxford University Press, Inc., 1917), p. 1014, on Matthew 13:11. Quoted by permission of Oxford University Press, Inc.

4 Paul Tillich, *Systematic Theology* (Chicago: University of Chicago Press, 1951), Vol. I, p. 109. Quoted by permission of the University of Chicago Press. On "mystery" see Tillich, *op. cit.*, pp. 108-117, 216, 217.

5 For illuminating, though differing views of the parables, see C. H. Dodd, *The Parables of the Kingdom* (New York: Charles Scribner's Sons, 1935) and Joachim Jeremias, *The Parables of Jesus* (London: Student Christian Movement, 1954).

6 David Morton, "Symbol," in *Ships in Harbour* (New York: G. P. Putnam's Sons, 1921), p. 30. Quoted by permission of David Morton.

7 On "paradox" Robert L. Calhoun once said: "A paradox is the putting together of two propositions which, for their full meaning, cannot stand alone, in isolation. It is therefore not a uniting of contradictions, for in contradictions the components can be distinguished and can stand alone. 'It thus does not stop the process of thought before it gets started, but rather leads thought on.' "

8 D. M. Baillie, *God Was in Christ,* 2d ed. (London: Faber and Faber Ltd., Publishers, 1948), p. 112. Quoted by permission of Professor D. M. Baillie.

9 Amelia Josephine Burr, "Certainty Enough," in *Selected Lyrics* (New York: Doubleday & Company, Inc., 1927), p. 21. Quoted by permission of Doubleday & Company, Inc.

I. GOD

Chapter 3. How Do We Know God?

1 Gustaf Aulén, *The Faith of the Christian Church* (Philadelphia: Muhlenberg Press, 1948), p. 32.
2 Reinhold Niebuhr, *Religion in Life,* 23 (1954), pp. 336, 337.
3 Jeremiah 33:2.
4 Jeremiah 33:4.
5 Luke 4:18.
6 Matthew 5:22, etc.

Chapter 4. The Nature of God

1 Genesis 17:1.
2 Genesis 31:42.
3 Genesis 49:24.
4 Genesis 31:42.
5 Genesis 32:9.
6 Exodus 3:15.
7 *Ibid.*
8 Exodus 3:14.
9 Isaiah 45:5.
10 Romans 15:6.
11 Matthew 6:9.
12 Mark 14:36.
13 Romans 8:15.
14 Isaiah 55:8, 9.
15 For a remarkable treatment and development of this point, see William Temple, *Nature, Man, and God* (London: Macmillan and Co., Ltd., 1934), Chs. 5, 11, 12.
16 Matthew 22:39.
17 Samuel F. Pugh in *The Christian-Evangelist,* March 28, 1951. Quoted by permission of the Editor.

Chapter 5. God and Nature

1 H. and H. A. Frankfort, John A. Wilson, Thorkild Jacobsen, William A. Irwin, *The Intellectual Adventure of Ancient Man,* an Oriental Institute Essay (Chicago: University of Chicago

Press, 1946), p. 224. Quoted by permission of the University of Chicago Press.

[2] *Ibid.,* p. 363. Also quoted by permission of the University of Chicago Press.

CHAPTER 6. GOD AND MAN

[1] Ecclesiastes 12:1; Isaiah 40:28; 43:15; Romans 1:25; I Peter 4:19.

[2] Harper and Brothers, 1942.

[3] Genesis 18:25; I Samuel 2:3; Psalm 7:11; 96:13; Hebrews 12:22, 23, 29.

[4] Psalm 19:14; Isaiah 41:14; 63:16.

[5] Daniel D. Williams, *What Present-Day Theologians Are Thinking* (New York: Harper and Brothers, 1952), p. 113. Quoted by permission of Harper and Brothers.

[6] Howard Thurman, *Meditations of the Heart* (New York: Harper and Brothers, 1953), p. 184. Quoted by permission of Harper and Brothers.

[7] I John 1:9.

[8] Romans 8:21.

CHAPTER 7. GOD AND THE REALM OF ACCIDENT

[1] Luke 13:4-5.

[2] Joseph W. Reeves in *The Pulpit,* August, 1950, p. 181. Copyrighted by the Christian Century Foundation and reprinted by permission of *The Pulpit.*

[3] See Gerald Heard, *A Preface to Prayer* (New York: Harper and Brothers, 1944), pp. 179-181.

CHAPTER 8. GOD AND EVIL

[1] I Kings 21:20; Psalm 52:3; Isaiah 59:7.

[2] Matthew 7:17; 12:35; Romans 12:9; I Thessalonians 5:22.

[3] Alfred E. Garvie in James Hastings, Ed., *Dictionary of the Apostolic Church,* 1916, Vol. I, p. 380.

[4] Genesis 1:31.

[5] Matthew 6:13.

[6] Luke 19:10; I John 1:7; Romans 8:1.

II. CHRIST

Chapter 9. God Was in Christ

[1] George A. Buttrick in *The Interpreter's Bible* (Nashville: Abingdon-Cokesbury Press, 1951), Vol. VII, p. 252.
[2] Mark 1:11 and Luke 3:22.
[3] Romans 1:3-4.
[4] John 1:1, 14.
[5] Roger Eddy Treat in Stanley I. Stuber and Thomas C. Clark, Eds., *Treasury of the Christian Faith* (New York: Association Press, 1949), pp. 392 f. Quoted by permission of Association Press.
[6] Luke 5:8.
[7] Matthew 16:16.

Chapter 10. The Only Son

[1] Hebrews 2:17.
[2] Hebrews 5:8.
[3] John 4:6.
[4] John 11:35.
[5] Mark 3:5.
[6] See Dale Moody, "God's Only Son; The Translation of John 3:16 in the Revised Standard Version," in *Journal of Biblical Literature,* 72 (1953), pp. 213-219.
[7] *Cf.* Hebrews 4:15.
[8] John 8:46.
[9] See E. D. Soper, *The Religions of Mankind,* rev. ed. (Nashville: Abingdon-Cokesbury Press, 1921), p. 302.
[10] Matthew 11:27.
[11] John 14:9.
[12] Christian F. Reisner in Stuber and Clark, Eds., *Treasury of the Christian Faith* (New York: Association Press, 1949), p. 395. Quoted by permission of Association Press.

Chapter 11. Christ and the Other Religions

[1] Matthew 12:30 and Luke 11:23.
[2] E. D. Soper, *The Religions of Mankind,* rev. ed. (Nashville: Abingdon-Cokesbury Press, 1921), p. 39. Quoted by permission of the Abingdon-Cokesbury Press.

[3] H. Kraemer, *The Christian Message in a Non-Christian World* (New York: Harper and Brothers, 1938), pp. 128 f.
[4] Mark 9:40; *cf.* Luke 9:50.
[5] Hebrews 1:1.
[6] Ephesians 4:13.
[7] A. J. Cronin, *The Keys of the Kingdom* (Boston: Little, Brown and Company, 1941), p. 320. Quoted by permission of Dr. A. J. Cronin.

Chapter 12. The Uniqueness of the Incarnation

[1] For yet other statements of this sort see Friedrich Heiler, "How Can Christian and Non-Christian Religions Co-operate?" in *The Hibbert Journal,* 52 (1954), pp. 107-118; and Joachim Wach, "General Revelation and the Religions of the World," in *The Journal of Bible and Religion,* 22 (1954), pp. 83-93.
[2] Clarence Tucker Craig, *The Beginning of Christianity* (Nashville: Abingdon-Cokesbury Press, 1943), p. 133. Quoted by permission of the Abingdon-Cokesbury Press.
[3] Harry Emerson Fosdick, *The Man from Nazareth as His Contemporaries Saw Him* (New York: Harper and Brothers, 1939), p. 234. Quoted by permission of Harper and Brothers.
[4] Mark 10:7, 8 and Matthew 19:5.
[5] Leviticus 19:18.

Chapter 13. The Acceptance and Rejection of Christ in the World

[1] Numbers 15:36; Joshua 7:25.
[2] Psalm 91:7; Deuteronomy 21:23.
[3] King James Version.
[4] Rudolf Bultmann, *Theology of the New Testament,* tr. by Kendrick Grobel (New York: Charles Scribner's Sons, 1951), Vol. I, p. 9. Quoted by permission of Charles Scribner's Sons.
[5] Rebecca E. Pitts in *The Hibbert Journal,* 51 (1952-1953), p. 244.

Chapter 14. The Miracles of Christ

[1] Howard Thurman, *Deep Is the Hunger* (New York: Harper and Brothers, 1951), p. 171. Quoted by permission of Harper and Brothers.
[2] John Knox, *Criticism and Faith* (Nashville: Abingdon-Cokesbury Press, 1952), p. 113. Quoted by permission of the Abingdon-Cokesbury Press.

3 Mark 1:21, 23, 29, 30, etc.

4 Matthew 8:8-10 and Luke 7:6-9; Matthew 11:4-5 and Luke 7:22; Matthew 12:27-28 and Luke 8:18-20; Matthew 12:43-45 and Luke 11:24-36.

5 Paul Tillich writes: "A genuine miracle is an event which is astonishing, unusual, shaking without contradicting the rational structure of reality. It is an event which points to the mystery of being, expressing its relation to us in a definite way. It is an occurrence which is received as a sign-event in an ecstatic experience. Only if these three conditions are fulfilled can one speak of a genuine miracle. This is emphasized in the synoptic records of the miracles of Jesus. Miracles are given only to those for whom they are sign-events, to those who receive them in faith. Jesus refuses to perform 'objective' miracles." (*Systematic Theology,* Vol. I, p. 117. Quoted by permission of the University of Chicago Press.) For further discussion of miracle, see Tillich, *op. cit.,* pp. 115-118.

6 Leslie D. Weatherhead, *Psychology, Religion and Healing* (London: Hodder and Stoughton Ltd., 1951), p. 43. Quoted by permission of Dr. Leslie D. Weatherhead.

7 S. Vernon McCasland, *By the Finger of God* (New York: The Macmillan Company, 1951), pp. 45, 95. Quoted by permission of The Macmillan Company.

8 For the relationship of miracle to the kingdom of God, see D. S. Cairns, *The Faith That Rebels,* 6th ed. (New York: Harper and Brothers, 1954).

9 See *Fortnight,* May 25, 1953.

10 By permission of Dr. Robert B. Munger.

11 For a popular but helpful treatment of miracle, see *Miracles* by C. S. Lewis (New York: The Macmillan Company, 1947).

Chapter 15. Why Did Jesus Die?

1 Luke 23:2.

2 Mark 3:21.

3 Mark 1:11, Matthew 3:17, and Luke 3:22.

4 Exodus 24:8.

5 Mark 14:24.

6 Romans 3:23.

7 Romans 1:18.

8 II Corinthians 5:21.

9 Frank Stagg, *The Cross—a Rationale,* p. 15. Quoted by permission of Frank Stagg, Professor of New Testament Interpretation, New Orleans Baptist Theological Seminary.

CHAPTER 16. THE RESURRECTION AND A NEW THEORY OF IMMORTALITY

1 Joseph B. Burgess, *Introduction to the History of Philosophy* (New York: McGraw-Hill Book Company, Inc., 1939), p. 530. Quoted by permission of the McGraw-Hill Book Company, Inc.
2 Henri Bergson, *Creative Evolution,* tr. by Arthur Mitchell (New York: Henry Holt and Company, Inc., 1911), pp. 270-271. Quoted by permission of Henry Holt and Company, Inc.
3 Lecomte du Noüy, *Human Destiny* (New York: Longmans, Green & Co., Inc., 1947), p. 87. Quoted by permission of Longmans, Green & Co., Inc.
4 Ovid R. Sellers, "Israelite Belief in Immortality," in *The Biblical Archaeologist,* VIII, 1 (Feb. 1945), p. 15. Quoted by permission of the McCormick Theological Seminary, Chicago.
5 Genesis 37:35; I Samuel 2:6; Isaiah 38:17, 18; Psalm 88:12; Isaiah 14:10.
6 Job 14:14; Isaiah 26:19; Psalm 73:24; Daniel 12:2. The Hebrew of Job 19:25, 26 is so difficult to translate that the meaning of that passage, which would otherwise be among those cited here, remains uncertain.
7 Luke 23:42-43.
8 John 11:25-26.
9 Philippians 1:23.
10 Lyman Abbott, *The Other Room* (New York: The Macmillan Company, 1904), p. 68. The quotations from this book are by permission of the author's estate, per Mr. Alexander L. Abbott.
11 *Ibid.,* p. 57.
12 Ralph W. Sockman, "Strength for Crises," in *Higher Happiness* (New York: Abingdon-Cokesbury Press, 1950), p. 62. Quoted by permission of Dr. Ralph W. Sockman.
13 John 11:11; Acts 7:60; I Thessalonians 4:15.
14 For a superb treatment of the issues in this chapter and the next, see John Baillie, *And the Life Everlasting* (New York: Charles Scribner's Sons, 1934). For a viewpoint differing somewhat from that of this chapter, see William Temple, *Nature, Man, and God* (1934), Ch. 18, "Moral and Religious Conditions of Eternal Life."

CHAPTER 17. HOW TO THINK ABOUT THE LAST JUDGMENT

1 Matthew 13:24-30, 47-49; 25:32-33.
2 Matthew 7:23.
3 William O. Douglas, *Of Men and Mountains* (New York: Harper and Brothers, 1950), p. 212. Quoted by permission of Harper and Brothers.

[4] John 3:19.
[5] Leslie D. Weatherhead, *When the Lamp Flickers* (Nashville: Abingdon-Cokesbury Press, 1948), p. 179. The excerpts from this book are quoted by permission of the Abingdon-Cokesbury Press.
[6] Revelation 20:12.
[7] Charles William Stubbs, "Conscience and Future Judgment," in James D. Morrison, *Masterpieces of Religious Verse* (New York: Harper and Brothers, 1948), p. 63, no. 194. By permission.
[8] *The Best of G. A. Studdert-Kennedy* (New York: Harper and Brothers, 1948), pp. 58, 61, 62f. Quoted by permission of Harper and Brothers.
[9] Leslie D. Weatherhead, *When the Lamp Flickers,* p. 182; cf. *After Death,* 2d ed., p. 68.
[10] Luke 19:10.
[11] Leslie D. Weatherhead, *When the Lamp Flickers,* p. 188; cf. *After Death,* p. 108.

III. THE CHURCH

Chapter 18. The Intention of Jesus for the Church

[1] Mark 14:24, Matthew 26:28, and Luke 22:20; I Corinthians 11:25.
[2] Jeremiah 31:33.
[3] Matthew 8:11 and Luke 13:29.
[4] Deuteronomy 31:30.
[5] Mark 12:30-31, Matthew 22:37-39, and Luke 10:27; Deuteronomy 6:5; Leviticus 19:18.
[6] Matthew 10:25; 5:11.
[7] Luke 12:32; Matthew 16:18.

Chapter 19. What Happened at Pentecost?

[1] Stewart Edward White, *The Betty Book* (New York: E. P. Dutton & Co., Inc., 1937), p. 248; Albert Payson Terhune, *Across the Line,* with notes and comments by Anice Terhune, and with a foreword by Rev. Dr. Joseph R. Sizoo of the Collegiate Church of St. Nicholas (New York: Dryden Press, 1945), p. 95.
[2] William Crookes in the *Quarterly Journal of Science,* July 1, 1871, quoted by Jean Burton, *Heyday of a Wizard, Daniel Home, the Medium* (New York: Alfred A. Knopf, Inc., 1944), p. 249.
[3] Leslie D. Weatherhead, *Psychology, Religion and Healing* (London: Hodder and Stoughton Ltd., 1951), p. 106.

[4] Carl Brumback, *What Meaneth This?* (Springfield, Mo.: The Gospel Publishing House, 1947).
[5] Matthew 18:19-20.

Chapter 20. The Essential Nature of the Church

[1] Lesslie Newbigin, *The Household of God* (New York: Friendship Press, 1954), p. 114.
[2] Luke 22:24; John 17:21; I Corinthians 1:10; Ephesians 4:4-6.
[3] Charles Clayton Morrison, *The Unfinished Reformation* (New York: Harper and Brothers, 1953), p. 157.
[4] Acts 2:44.
[5] I Corinthians 13:8; 14:18.
[6] Morrison, *The Unfinished Reformation,* p. 194.

Chapter 21. The Meaning of Baptism

[1] Carl H. Kraeling, *John the Baptist* (New York: Charles Scribner's Sons, 1951), p. 97. Quoted by permission of Charles Scribner's Sons.
[2] John 3:23.
[3] Acts 8:36, 38.
[4] Joachim Jeremias, *Die Wiederentdeckung von Bethesda* (Göttingen: Vandenhoeck and Ruprecht, 1949), p. 24.
[5] Acts 2:38.
[6] Acts 16:33.
[7] Karl Barth, *Die kirchliche Lehre von der Taufe* (Theologische Studien herausgegeben von Karl Barth, Heft 14), 3d ed. (Zollikon-Zürich: Evangelischer Verlag A. G., 1947), p. 3, tr. by Jack Finegan.
[8] *Ibid.,* pp. 30, 40.
[9] *The Christian-Evangelist,* March 29, 1950, p. 294.
[10] Titus 3:5.
[11] Romans 6:4.
[12] *Op. cit.,* pp. 3-5.
[13] For a different view of baptism from that presented in this chapter see Oscar Cullmann, *Baptism in the New Testament,* tr. by J. K. S. Reid (London: Student Christian Movement Press, Ltd., 1952). Also, for a helpful critique of various views, see John Baillie, *What Is Christian Civilization?* (New York: Charles Scribner's Sons, 1945), Appendix A, pp. 71-86, "Kierkegaard, Barth, and Brunner on the Practice of Baptism."

Chapter 22. The Significance of the Lord's Supper

1 Acts 2:46; I Corinthians 10:16, Revised Standard Version margin; Luke 22:19 contains the Greek word for giving thanks from which "eucharist" is derived; I Corinthians 11:20.
2 Exodus 12:6, Revised Standard Version margin.
3 Josephus, *Jewish War,* VI. ix. 3.
4 Mark 14:12, Matthew 26:17, and Luke 22:8.
5 Mark 14:2 and Matthew 26:5.
6 For a different view see Joachim Jeremias, *Die Abendmahlsworte Jesu* (Göttingen: Vandenhoeck and Ruprecht, 1935).
7 I Corinthians 11:21-22.
8 Justin Martyr, *Apology,* 65-67.
9 Luke 24:35.
10 I Corinthians 11:26.

Chapter 23. The Hope of the Church

1 Norman Thomas as quoted in *Time,* Pacific Edition, March 2, 1953, p. 24.
2 Mark 13:33.
3 Matthew 6:10.
4 Luke 17:21.
5 Revelation 20:4.
6 Revelation 20:11; 21:1.
7 Revelation 21:4.
8 Luke 11:20 and Matthew 12:28; Luke 11:31 and Matthew 12:42.
9 C. H. Dodd, *The Coming of Christ* (New York, American Branch: Cambridge University Press, 1951), pp. 20-21. Quoted by permission of the Cambridge University Press.
10 I Peter 1:3.
11 II Corinthians 4:8-9, 14.